Praise for *The Friendly Vegan Cookbook*

"Tie up your apron and dance in the kitchen while you cook up these insanely delish dishes that celebrate the power of plants! From the tofu ricotta stuffed shells drizzled with flavorful tomato sauce to the slurpable noodle soups, you won't want to stop cooking from this inspired collection of recipes that show that a kind kitchen should come with no sacrifice—only joy."

—Daniella Monet, actress and singer starring in Nickelodeon's *Victorious*

"Eating vegan should be FUN! These wonderful dishes are a celebration of delicious food and the experience of sharing nourishing meals with loved ones. *The Friendly Vegan Cookbook* will become a staple in so many kitchens!"

—Mýa, Grammy award-winning artist

"There is a unique pressure that comes with cooking plant-based meals for non-vegan friends and it can feel like your guests' entire perception of vegan food depends on your cooking skills—a tall order! But with *The Friendly Vegan Cookbook*, and Toni and Michelle's expert guidance and inspiration, impressing your guests will come easy to you! Just be ready to act humble when everyone's minds are blown by these incredible dishes."

—Evanna Lynch, actress appearing in the Harry Potter film series

"*The Friendly Vegan Cookbook* is the perfect starting point for anyone wanting to go vegan or add more plant-based foods into their diet. The recipes are easy-to-make, the book is chock-full of great tips, and Michelle and Toni are incredibly upbeat and charming. *The Friendly Vegan Cookbook* should grace everyone's plant-based cookbook collection."

—Colleen Holland, publisher of *VegNews*

"Toni and Michelle's mission to create a more plant-forward world is hugely inspirational. This book is packed with delicious and easy plant-based recipes that will inspire you to make kinder, healthier and more environmentally friendly food choices. The future is vegan, join us!"

—Robbie Lockie, cofounder of *Plant Based News*

"Food should be a means for connection and community—but it can be tricky to satisfy everyone at the table. *The Friendly Vegan Cookbook* will help you do just that, while demonstrating that plant-based meals are satisfying, familiar, and delicious!"

—Colleen Patrick-Goudreau, author of *The Joy of Vegan Baking* and *The 30-Day Vegan Challenge*

"This fantastic cookbook shows how you can be a friend to animals while also being a good friend to your human companions. Cook up these perfected plant-based recipes and share them with friends as often as you can!"

—Gene Baur, cofounder of Farm Sanctuary

"Adopting a plant-based diet is the single most impactful action an individual can take to reduce their carbon footprint!"

—Aidan Gallagher, United Nations Environment Programme Goodwill Ambassador, North America

THE
Friendly Vegan
COOKBOOK

Also by Toni Okamoto

Plant-Based on a Budget
The Super Easy Vegan Slow Cooker Cookbook

Also Available from the Authors

The Plant-Powered People Podcast | PlantPoweredPodcast.com

Plant-Based Meal Plans | PlantBasedMealPlan.com

7 Days Documentary | 7DaysDoc.com

Vegan YouTube Videos | YouTube.com/WorldofVegan

Budget Vegan Recipes | PlantBasedonaBudget.com

Food & Lifestyle Website | WorldofVegan.com

THE
Friendly Vegan
COOKBOOK

100 Essential Recipes to Share with Vegans and Omnivores Alike

MICHELLE CEHN & TONI OKAMOTO

BenBella Books, Inc.
Dallas, TX

This book, dear reader, is dedicated to you. We are profoundly honored and so very grateful that you opened your heart, your mind, and your kitchen, and invited us in to share recipes and ideas that were created to do just that: bring people together. Food has the power not only to nourish us and bring us comfort, but to bridge the divides that separate us. Our hope is that *The Friendly Vegan Cookbook* will bring joy and conviviality to your table, and help you sow seeds of compassion with every meal shared with family, friends, and strangers alike. You always have a friend in us!

Contents

DRINKS

DIY STAPLES

FRIENDLY VEGAN MENUS   261

Foreword

When I won first place on Food Network's television show *Cup-cake Wars* with my entirely plant-based cupcakes nearly a decade ago, nobody could believe it. It was a time when *tofu* really was a four-letter word. Today, demand for vegan food—including our poor old friend tofu—is booming, largely because of how delicious vegan fare has become.

As the author of four best-selling vegan cookbooks, I've seen firsthand the powerful impact that providing delicious recipes can have on individuals and families looking to move away from the "standard American diet" and toward meals that are more plant-based. At the same time, we have almost too much of a good thing. With so many vegan resources available, it can be tough to know what recipes will actually produce good results—something amazing that you and your friends will want to share.

It's been exciting to watch Toni and Michelle as we've all worked in different ways to show the world just how palate pleasing plant-powered eating can be. What I, and so many others, really appreciate most about Michelle and Toni is their genuine, enthusiastic, and fun personalities and their nonjudgmental, welcoming approach to vegan food. Even from afar, reading their blogs, watching their videos, listening to their podcast, and exploring their recipes really make you feel like you're in a room among friends.

In this new book, prepare to be wowed by just how simple it is to make your favorites into vegan delights you can enjoy for years to come. That includes classic dishes like fettuccine Alfredo and shepherd's pie, new favorites like veganized toaster pastries, and even creative ways to dress up your BFF, tofu.

Vegan eating has come far in the twenty-first century. I'm grateful to Toni and Michelle for helping to show us the way. What a time to be alive, when doing the right thing also means doing what's just delicious!

Chloe Coscarelli

Introduction

Hi, friends! We're so excited that you've welcomed us into your kitchen. Spatula cheers!

Before we jump in, let us just say: we *loooove* food. And not just healthy stuff like smoothie bowls and salads. We love *all* food. Pizza, and burgers, and pot pies, and chowder, and sushi, and soft serve, and cookies, and . . . well, all the foods we've included in this book!

When we first became vegan more than a decade ago, we thought that being vegan would mean life without many of these dishes. After all, how can you have ooey-gooey cheese without dairy? Or juicy burgers without beef? Or cookies that don't crumble apart without eggs?

Oh my goodness, were we wrong! You can absolutely have it all—and it can taste even better than you remember—without a single animal product in sight. And that's what we're going to show you in this book: how to prepare and enjoy vegan food, without any sacrifices!

Of course, there's a lot of not-so-great vegan food out there. Many of the recipes we've made over the years ended up as dramatic fails. Grainy fettuccine Alfredo, pumpkin pie that spilled all over the oven when we took it out, creamy soup that curdled—ugh. Was this what plant-based life was going to be like?

No way! Plant-based food has come a long way since those early days. Today, there are more vegan cookbooks than you can count. But we felt something was missing. While cookbooks are being released faster than we can spell T-O-F-U, they seem to be getting farther and farther away from what our friends and family really need: familiar, perfected, un-mess-up-able staples that are tasty enough to share with your self-proclaimed carnivorous neighbor. So that's exactly what we set out to create.

This book has been in our hearts for a long time. It's the book we wish had existed when we first became vegan, and one that we've felt passionate about bringing to life for many years to help make the plant-powered journey more enjoyable, vibrant, and fun for all those who embark on it.

This book carries with it recipes, stories, and inspiration from each of us and our journeys (both separate and together).

Before we jump in, we'd love to share a bit about why we're here as your guides.

Meet Your Guides

Michelle Cehn

I grew up like most other kids in America—eating pasta loaded with Parmesan cheese, gobbling cereal drenched in cow's milk, and making occasional trips to fast-food spots for some chicken nuggets (which I wanted *just* for the free toy). All that changed when I turned eight and decided to become vegetarian, and later vegan.

For a long time, my diet was far from perfect. I had no idea how to prepare plant-based food, and the specialty products back then (like vegan meats and cheeses) were hard to find and not that good. I ate a lot of "accidentally vegan" ramen noodles, cereal with soy milk, salad, and bland pasta with olive oil.

It took years of trial and error in the kitchen, following countless recipes that turned out well only some of the time, before my eyes were opened to the vast and varied world of plant-powered possibilities. I began to explore more fruits, vegetables, and ingredients I had never even heard of before (hi, nutritional yeast!). I slowly learned how to cook and how to transform plant-based food into mouthwatering feasts—even beyond what I had experienced before I went vegan.

As the food in my own kitchen became creative, rich, flavorful, and tasty enough to wow even my most die-hard meat-loving friends and family, I became passionate about helping others eliminate that period of struggle that so often accompanies diet change and learning what to eat and how to cook in new ways. And that's how World of Vegan, the website I founded, was born; how Toni and I found one another; and why I'm writing this cookbook today.

Toni Okamoto

When I first became vegan, I was so excited to finally give it a try after a couple of years of being vegetarian, and I couldn't wait to tell my parents. My dad reacted by calling me a "hippie weed smoker" (which is funny because I've never smoked weed, and it has nothing to do with food). But the experience was representative of the obstacles that would follow my decision to change my diet. I realized that it wasn't a choice that was going to affect just *me*— it was also going to be a transition for my family, friends, coworkers, anyone I dated, and everyone with whom I shared food. People had misconceptions about what being a vegan meant, and sometimes even a negative association with the word *vegan*.

So, in my twelve years of vegan living, I've found that the best way to win the support and understanding of friends and family is to be a friendly vegan. I've wanted to positively and kindly introduce my loved ones to the best vegan foods and to slowly and respectfully, over long periods of time, share why I'm so passionate about what they had considered simply a "diet." And I'm so grateful that this approach has led to successful outcomes, with most of the people in my life (even the biggest naysayers) choosing more plant-based options or even fully embracing a vegetarian lifestyle. It takes time and patience, but knowing that my parents, on their own, choose Soy-rizo over chorizo (sausage) makes it worth the wait.

I've carried this approach over to my website, Plant-Based on a Budget, and it has been important to me to maintain a culture across my platforms that welcomes anyone who wants to save money while eating healthier and plant-based. And to me, this book is an extension of that. Teaming up with Michelle—an amazing, compassionate friend—and creating this inclusive resource has been a dream of mine, and I'm overjoyed that it's now a reality.

Becoming Your Guides

The start of our friendship was unconventional. Michelle was living in Oak-land and Toni was living in Sacramento (an hour and a half away), yet despite the distance, Toni knew we should be friends. We were about the same age, we were both committed to helping animals and passionate about vegan living, we both loved creating content online, and we just seemed like an obvious match.

Toni messaged Michelle, asking if she could come hang out with her sometime, but surprisingly, Michelle told Toni that she was so focused on work and World of Vegan that she didn't have time to hang out with friends.

Toni suggested that instead of hanging out like normal people (like going to the movies, getting coffee, or eating at a restaurant), we could work together creating content. And that's how we built our friendship—helping people become and stay vegan.

Since then, we've created hundreds of YouTube videos together, co-directed a mini-documentary called *7 Days*, produced *The Plant-Powered People Podcast*, written the Plant-Based on a Budget Meal Plans (which have helped thousands of people), and developed a truly meaningful and valuable partnership. But the most important thing we've built together is a community and culture that is truly nonjudgmental and welcomes all people, regardless of where they are on their plant-based journeys. So, dear reader, we thank you for bringing us along on *your* journey, and we promise to be your gracious hosts and steadfast companions throughout.

Your Friendly Vegan Cookbook

Together, we've been vegan for more than two decades. We came from totally different paths in life, but the two things we've found both individually and as a duo are the power of being friendly and the power of sharing good food. There's nothing like a plate of Challah French Toast (page 39) dripping with maple syrup or a bowl of hearty Yellow Tofu Curry (page 66) infused with Southeast Asian spices to instantly quiet the naysayers, bring the focus away from dietary differences, and stop the tiresome questions about where we get our protein. Instead of being combative and pushing our food choices on those around us, we've learned that being happy, friendly, nonjudgmental individuals is the greatest (and most effective) way to inspire positive change. Gathering around the table to share a fresh, flavorful home-cooked meal that's familiar and comforting has the power to transform perceptions about what plant-based food is all about. With this book, we've taken the pain out of meal preparation and the struggle out of changing the way you eat, to bring forth the flavors, comfort, familiarity, and ease of cooking so you and your loved ones can enjoy and celebrate one of life's great joys: food.

And so, after countless recipe fails (and wins!), this cookbook—a collection of our go-to fail-proof recipes that taste as good as (or better than) the originals—was born. You won't find weird flours, hard-to-find ingredients, or vegetables you've never heard of in these pages. Instead, you'll discover recipes that you'll be eager to share with friends, that will make your taste buds sing and have you going back for seconds, and that will fill your house with tantalizing aromas whether you're preparing a simple post-work meal or an elaborate holiday feast.

To fine-tune our recipes to appeal to the die-hard meat eaters, vegetarians, and vegans among us, we turned to nearly one hundred recipe testers of all ages and cooking skill levels from all around the world. With their help, each recipe in this collection has been refined and perfected, with an emphasis on maximizing flavor and minimizing fuss. If you're a fan of easy-to-prepare food that looks and smells as delightful as it tastes, this book is our gift to you.

Choosing vegan *doesn't* mean self-denial. Quite the opposite. Choosing vegan means a whole new world of plant-powered ingredients opening up to you. It means getting out of old food ruts and finding a new sense of creativity in the kitchen. It means discovering new flavors, spices, and cooking techniques. It means feeling that flush of excitement when you make a plant-based lasagna stuffed with vegan ricotta and smothered in a zesty marinara, and it tastes even *better* than the one you grew up with. It means enjoying food *even more*.

And beyond our amazing tried-and-tested recipes, there's so much more that we want to share with you to make your plant-based journey easier and more enjoyable.

If you picked up this cookbook and are ready to get cooking but aren't completely sure where you'll be getting your protein without meat, we've got you! And if you're prepping your plant-powered kitchen for the first time and don't know what staples to buy, we're here to help.

We've spent over ten years (each!) supporting fledgling vegans and seasoned herbivores alike with their questions about plant-based living, and have created resources that show you

- How to go vegan
- What tools you need to outfit your kitchen
- How to stock your pantry
- How to save time and money in the kitchen
- Plant-based nutrition basics
- Our favorite vegan versions of milk, cheese, ice cream, and beyond

Even after you've tried every recipe in this book, we're still here for you. At FriendlyVeganCookbook.com, you'll find more helpful resources, new recipes, and fun videos we created to continue inspiring and motivating you.

But for now, while you have your nose in this book, let's do what we came here to do and get cooking! We're excited to share these dishes we know will delight your taste buds and dazzle your friends and family, so grab your apron and join us in the kitchen.

And if you snap any photos in the kitchen, please make sure to tag @vegan, @plantbasedonabudget, and #friendlyvegan on Instagram. We love seeing and sharing your photos!

♥ *Michelle and Toni*

Prepping Your Plant-Powered Kitchen

Good news! You probably have a lot of the basics in your kitchen already. Pasta, rice, beans, and other familiar pantry staples are the foundations of many of the delicious meals we'll be showing you in this book.

But there are a few key ingredients popping up in multiple recipes that may be unfamiliar to you. If the word "nooch" makes you raise your eyebrows, then you'll find this section especially informative! Consider it your "vegucation." First, we'll cover the fresh foods and dry staples to keep on hand, then introduce you to the kitchen equipment you'll need to make these fantastic recipes.

Stocking Your Pantry

With a well-stocked pantry, one thing is assured: you'll never go hungry! When you invest in staples like rice, beans, and vegetable bouillon, and keep your kitchen stocked with onions and garlic, it's easy to whip together dishes both sweet and savory, from Chewy Chocolate Peanut Butter Granola Bars (page 49) to Cornbread Chili Casserole (page 82). These are some of our most often used ingredients:

Dry Goods

Chocolate chips (vegan)

Flour (all-purpose)

Ground flaxseed meal

Nutritional yeast

Panko bread crumbs

Pasta (all shapes and sizes)

Quinoa

Raw almonds

Raw cashews

Rice

Sugar (brown, granulated, and powdered)

Textured vegetable protein (TVP)

Vegetable bouillon

Bottled and Canned Goods

Almond extract

Apple cider vinegar

Canned beans (assorted varieties)

Canola oil

Extra-virgin olive oil

Hot sauce (we love Sriracha)

Ketchup

Mustard (Dijon and yellow)

Peanut butter

Rice vinegar

Soy sauce

Toasted sesame oil

Vanilla extract

Vegetable shortening

Dried Herbs and Spices

Basil

Bay leaves

Black pepper

Black salt (kala namak)

Chili powder

Cinnamon

Cumin

Garlic powder

Marjoram

Nutmeg

Oregano

Poultry seasoning

Red chili pepper flakes

Salt

Smoked paprika

Thyme

Turmeric

Fruits and Veggies

Avocados

Bananas

Bell peppers

Carrots

Celery

Frozen fruit (assorted varieties)

Frozen veggies (assorted varieties)

Garlic

Mushrooms

Onions

Potatoes

Tomatoes

Zucchini

Refrigerated Items

Plant-based milk

Tofu

Vegan butter (sticks are ideal for easy measuring)

Vegan mayo

Five Superstar Vegan Ingredients

When you step into the world of vegan cooking, it can be overwhelming to see fifteen different plant-based milk options or to read a recipe calling for ingredients you've never heard of. To make it easier for you, let us introduce some of our favorite staple ingredients that may be new to you.

Black Salt (Kala Namak): We turn to black salt when we want to achieve an "eggy" flavor in a dish, such as Tofu Scramble (page 22) or Stephanie's Deviled Potatoes (page 141). Black salt (which isn't actually black and is usually pale pink) has a sulfury flavor and smell that's very reminiscent of eggs. Skeptical? Trust us—it really lifts these recipes up a notch.

Ground Flaxseed Meal: Ground flaxseed meal (also known as flaxmeal) is another staple vegan ingredient that we turn to often as an egg replacer in our recipes. When mixed with water or another liquid and allowed to sit for a few minutes, flaxseed meal will gel and function as an effective binder in baked goods. It's also rich in omega-3s and packed with fiber and protein. We always keep a stash in our refrigerators.

Nutritional Yeast: Also affectionately referred to as "nooch" or "vegan fairy dust," nutritional yeast is an essential ingredient in any plant-based kitchen. Whether purchased prepackaged or from the bulk section at your local natural-foods store, you'll find that these dry yellow flakes impart a savory, cheesy flavor to vegan mac 'n' cheese, tofu scrambles, pesto, stuffed shells, and beyond.

Plant-Based Milk: It can be pretty overwhelming to visit the plant-based milk section at the grocery store since it's exploding with options. For the most part, you can use unsweetened, plain plant-based milk in our recipes, but we've made sure to specify if another milk will work better. You're welcome to choose the base of the milk that you'd like (soy, almond, oat, cashew, etc.), but we believe that soy milk works the best due to its high protein content, creaminess, and neutral flavor. You can also make your own milk from scratch in minutes—check out our recipe for DIY Almond Milk (page 224).

Vegetable Bouillon: Vegetable bouillon is one of our favorite ingredients. It's essentially condensed soup stock that comes in the form of little cubes or as a powder in jars. Having it on hand makes it convenient and easy to prepare soups and sauces. In any of our recipes that call for vegetable broth, you're welcome to use the equivalent amount of bouillon and water instead. Better Than Bouillon is one of our go-to brands; it comes in recyclable glass jars, and a single container makes thirty-eight servings.

All About Tofu

Tofu is one of the most misunderstood plant-based ingredients. Until we started food blogs, we thought tofu was weird and bland. But once we got to know this healthy protein made from soybeans, we both quickly fell in love. Tofu can be transformed into so many things. Ricotta. Mousse. Meats. "Egg" scramble. Pie filling. The possibilities are endless!

But before you run to the store looking for tofu, it's important to understand the different types, as each behaves quite differently from the next in cooking. The two that we use most often are extra-firm tofu and silken tofu. In the refrigerator section at grocery stores, you can find tofu packaged in water, pressed tofu that's vacuum packed, and even marinated baked tofu. Shelf-stable tofu packaged in aseptic boxes is often stocked in the unrefrigerated Asian section of the supermarket.

Extra-Firm and Super-Firm Tofu: This is the tofu we use most often. Its dense texture makes it easy to slice, dice, and crumble, and it doesn't fall apart as easily as other varieties do while cooking. We use this in recipes including our Tofu Scramble (page 22), Rainbow Tofu Kebabs (page 134), and Tofu Bacon (page 234). Super-firm tofu is technically even more dense and firm than extra-firm tofu, but we use these interchangeably in all our recipes.

Silken Tofu: Also called "soft tofu," this is an extremely delicate, high-moisture-content tofu that can be blended to create creamy dishes, especially desserts. We use this in our Chocolate Mousse (page 199), Pumpkin Chocolate Pie (page 176), Challah French Toast (page 39), and Fudge Pops (page 200)—all recipes that you'd *never* guess are made with tofu. Like extra-firm tofu, silken tofu loses any "beany" flavor when seasoned or blended with other ingredients.

Tofu Pressing

Pressing your extra-firm tofu removes excess water so that the tofu better absorbs the flavor of marinades and seasonings and eliminates excess liquid in a recipe. It also enables the tofu to crisp up better during cooking. If you don't have time for pressing your tofu, simply wrap it in a kitchen towel and squeeze out excess liquid with your hands over the sink.

Although neither of us has ever owned one, a tofu press is a kitchen gadget worth considering. You can also use items you probably already own as a DIY tofu press. After removing tofu from its package, wrap it in a clean kitchen towel, place it on a rimmed plate or pan, and top with a heavy pot of water or stack of books. Allow it to sit for 5 to 10 minutes before using it in a recipe.

Kitchen Equipment

Cooking is a million times easier when you have the right tools, and investing in our recommended equipment will make your experience in the kitchen much more efficient and fun. Here are some of the tools we use in our book, listed from the things we can't live without to the items that are just nice to have.

Chef's Knife: A large, sharp, high-quality (and well-cared-for) knife is number one on our list. Many people have an entire block of knives, but 90 percent of your cutting and slicing can be done with a single chef's knife. If you struggle to cut a tomato with a clean slice, your knife could use a sharpening (or an upgrade). Treat yoself!

Pots (Small/Medium and Large): An essential for *any* kitchen. We both use 2-quart and 3-quart pots regularly. And, as you'll notice in our recipes, we love making huge batches of soup! This requires a large soup pot for maximum soupage. We both use 8-quart pots for that.

Large Nonstick Skillet with a Glass Lid: This is a staple for stir-fries, tofu scrambles, and beyond. The lid is needed for a few of our favorite recipes, including Mexican Rice (page 161).

Microwave: Microwaves are handy for melting chocolate without a double boiler and for reheating leftovers fast without the oven.

Measuring Cups and Measuring Spoons: Our recipes are measured in cups, tablespoons, and teaspoons, so a nice set of measuring cups and spoons are essential for making the recipes in this book. You can even find some good sets at your local dollar store.

Blender: A blender is central to most vegan kitchens—not only for smoothies but also for creamy sauces, cheeses, and blended soups. If you're able to invest in a high-powered blender, it will pay off for years to come. We both use a Vitamix and believe it is totally worth the investment.

Baking Pans or Sheet Pans: Any baking pans will do, but our favorites are aluminum commercial baker's half-sheet pans. Two is all you'll ever need, and when cared for, they can last a lifetime.

Silicone Baking Mat: Silicone mats have totally changed the baking game. No longer will you have to worry about your cookies or veggies sticking to the pan, nor will you need to get your hands slimy buttering the baking sheet. You'll also use less butter or oil, making recipes a tad healthier, and you'll save money by not having to purchase parchment paper so often.

Cake Pans: You can find these in any size, but we recommend 8-inch pans as a nice standard. If you foresee baking layer cakes, it's handy to get two or three so you can bake all the layers at once. And if you want to make our Birthday Cake (page 170), you'll need three cake pans! You can also invest in a cake leveler if you'll be making multitiered cakes. This helps create a flat top that looks beautiful and professional when frosted.

Springform Pan: For our Ice Cream Cake (page 191), we call for a springform pan to make the process much easier. This pan allows you to release the cake in its original form without damaging it.

Cupcake/Muffin Pans: Essential for cupcakes and muffins, of course!

Cupcake Liners: We have a little drawer in each of our kitchens where we stash cupcake liners, sprinkles, and pastry bags and piping tips (for decorating with frosting). Not all of these are essential, but cupcake liners are always useful to keep on hand. You'll also need them for making our Peanut Butter Cups (page 207).

Pastry Bags and Piping Tips: These will help your baked goods look like treats straight from a bakery. You can substitute a plastic bag with a corner cut off instead, but your cupcakes, cakes, and deviled eggs won't look quite as refined as they would with professional piping tips (which you can get for just a few dollars). You can also buy reusable silicone pastry bags to cut back on plastic waste.

Donut Pan: If you'd like to make our delicious Donuts (page 189), you'll need a standard-sized nonstick donut pan.

Ramekins: It's handy to have some extra-small bowls, also known as ramekins, for heating or mixing very small portions.

Food Processor: A food processor is another kitchen essential used throughout this book. It is a magical tool that can shred, slice, chop, mix, and purée ingredients, and it will save you both time and energy.

Immersion Blender: You can get away without an immersion blender (we both did for many years), but it does make life easier when you're making creamy soups. Instead of having to dump hot soup into a blender, you can pop the little immersion blender straight into the hot pot on the stove and give it a whirl. It is inexpensive, relatively small, and easy to store in your kitchen.

Nut Milk Bag: True, many people go through life unaware that nut milk bags even exist. But in a plant-powered kitchen, they're extremely handy. You'll use these to make your own nut milk in minutes, and for recipes like our Fettuccine Alfredo (page 75) and Horchata (page 214). They cost just a few dollars and take up almost no space. You can order them online or find them at many natural food stores.

Waffle Iron: Our Waffles (page 29) are crunchy on the outside, soft on the inside, and perfect for Sunday brunches, and to make them, you're going to need a waffle iron.

Popsicle Molds: To make our Fudge Pops (page 200), it's helpful to have popsicle molds. You can get them pretty much anywhere during the summer, and online all year round. In a pinch, you can use an Okamoto family hack:

pour the mixture into an ice cube tray, cover the tray with aluminum foil, and stick toothpicks into each cube before freezing.

Sushi Mat: If you plan on making sushi regularly, we recommend a sushi mat. It makes the rolling process much easier, creating a tighter, cleaner roll. If you don't have one, you can also use your hands to roll your sushi like a burrito.

How to Melt Chocolate

Double Boiler: The surest way to melt chocolate is to use a double boiler (or makeshift double boiler) because you can watch and constantly stir the chocolate as it melts—so you're less likely to burn and ruin the chocolate. To make your own double boiler, fill a pot with 1 or 2 inches of water and place over medium heat on the stove. Place a smaller heat-proof bowl over the pot, put the chocolate in the bowl, and allow the steam to melt the chocolate while stirring frequently.

Microwave: In a small microwave-safe bowl, microwave the chocolate for 30 seconds. Mix with a fork until smooth. If the chocolate is still lumpy, microwave for additional 20-second intervals, mixing in between each, until the chocolate is completely smooth.

Note: Chocolate is sensitive to heat and can seize up and harden if you aren't careful. Once the chocolate seizes, it's no longer usable in our recipes.

Okay, friends. We've now prepared you with the basics that you need to stock your pantry and your kitchen, and throughout this book you'll find many more of our tips for how to prepare food in the most efficient and tasty ways possible.

Breakfast & Brunch

Fluffy French toast, savory veggie scrambles, wholesome bowls of crunchy granola . . . What would mornings be without breakfast? Whether you need something quick and easy to eat on the go or crave comfort-food favorites for a leisurely weekend brunch, we've got recipes to suit every occasion and palate.

If you've never made Tofu Scramble (page 22) before, we suggest starting with this classic—our favorite go-to meal when we're craving a savory breakfast. It's packed with protein, and you can make a big batch that will last throughout the week. If you're feeling fancy, you can serve it up with a side of our restaurant-style Avocado Toast (page 25) and a refreshing Mango Smoothie (page 56). (We know, it sounds basic *and it is*, but it's also crazy good!) But let's be real, we love *all* these recipes, and know you'll enjoy exploring these scrumptious morning meal possibilities, too. Bon appétit!

Tofu Scramble

This garlicky, easy-to-prepare scramble is loaded with flavor and protein to help you feel sated all the way until lunchtime. When we introduced this savory dish to Michelle's birth father after he first became vegan, he started eating it for breakfast nearly *every single day*. If you, too, get hooked, keep it interesting by adding it to our Breakfast Burrito (page 26).

Yield: 2 large portions or 4 sides

Prep time: 10 minutes | Cook time: 14 minutes | Total time: 24 minutes

1 tablespoon canola or vegetable oil

½ red or green bell pepper, diced

½ medium yellow or red onion, diced

4 medium cloves garlic, minced

1 (16-ounce) block extra-firm tofu, pressed

1½ teaspoons ground turmeric

1½ tablespoons vegan butter

2 tablespoons nutritional yeast

½ teaspoon salt or black salt (kala namak), plus additional for serving, to taste

½ teaspoon ground black pepper, plus additional for serving, to taste

2 tablespoons sliced chives, for garnish

Hot sauce, for serving, to taste (optional)

1. In a large pan over medium heat, heat the oil. Add the bell pepper, onion, and garlic, and sauté for 5 to 7 minutes, stirring occasionally, until the bell pepper and onion are tender.

2. Using your fingers, crumble the tofu into the pan.

3. Add the turmeric, vegan butter, nutritional yeast, salt, and pepper to the tofu and veggies and mix thoroughly. Cook for 5 to 7 minutes, stirring occasionally, until thoroughly mixed and heated. If you like, top the scramble with additional salt and pepper, sliced chives, and hot sauce.

My Tips

Friendly Suggestion: This is a great recipe for when you want to clean out your refrigerator. Feel free to add extra veggies like spinach, asparagus (cut into 1-inch pieces), cherry tomatoes, chopped mushrooms, or whatever you have on hand. This is also a great way to add color and nutrition to the dish.

Avocado Toast

This is one of those trends that should *never* go out of style. Toni loves avocados *so much* that her husband hid her engagement ring in an avocado when he proposed during their weekly trip to the farmers' market. The only thing greater than a perfect avocado is one with a sparkly ring inside! It's no surprise: she said yes, and they were saying their "I do's" four months later! During their wedding, Paul was said to be the avocado to her toast. Toni and Paul, this decadent avo toast is for you.

Yield: 1–2 servings

Prep time: 5 minutes | Total time: 8 minutes

1 (4-inch) piece sourdough baguette, sliced down the middle to create 2 open-faced pieces

Drizzle of extra-virgin olive oil

½ perfectly ripe large avocado, pitted and peeled

Pinch of chunky sea salt

Pinch of cracked black pepper

Pinch of garlic powder

Pinch of red chili pepper flakes

1–2 small handfuls sprouts, arugula, or microgreens

4–6 cherry tomatoes, halved or quartered

Pinch of black sesame seeds (optional)

1. Toast the slices of sourdough baguette in a toaster or toaster oven until golden brown.
2. Drizzle the toasted bread with the olive oil.
3. Mash half of the avocado on each slice of bread, spreading it evenly across the face of the bread.
4. Sprinkle with the sea salt, cracked black pepper, garlic powder, and red chili pepper flakes.
5. Top with the greens, cherry tomatoes, and black sesame seeds (if using), and enjoy immediately.

My Tips

Avocado-Saving Tip: How many times have you lost a precious (and expensive) avocado because it overripened before you had a chance to eat it? We've been there—but no more! When you buy avocados, allow them to ripen on the counter. As soon as they're ripe, pop them in the fridge (unopened) and they will remain in that perfectly ripe, buttery state for more than a week. Magic!

Breakfast Burrito

We often double our Tofu Scramble recipe (page 22) just so we have enough left over to make into a breakfast burrito the next day. This is an incredibly versatile and delicious breakfast that can be personalized in limitless ways—just take a good look in your fridge and use what you have on hand, from jarred olives or capers to leftover beans or rice. It's quick to make when the scramble has already been prepared, and can even be packed up and eaten on the go.

Yield: 1 burrito

Prep time: 10 minutes | Cook time: 5 minutes | Total time: 15 minutes

1 teaspoon vegetable oil
⅔ cup leftover Tofu
   Scramble (page 22)
1 small handful fresh
   spinach
1 large flour tortilla
Dollops of guacamole
   (the more the merrier)
   or ½ ripe avocado,
   pitted and sliced
¼ cup Pico de Gallo
   (page 242)

Optional Add-ins:

2 tablespoons packed
   thinly sliced green
   onions
Salsa or hot sauce
Cooked vegan bacon
   (store-bought or from
   the recipe on page 234)
Dollop of Nacho Cheese
   Sauce (page 137)
Sautéed sliced
   mushrooms
Sautéed soy chorizo or
   vegan beefy crumbles
Vegan cheese shreds

1. In a small nonstick sauté pan over medium-high heat, heat the vegetable oil, leftover tofu scramble, and spinach and sauté until warmed through.

2. Warm the tortilla over a flame on the stove, in a pan, or in the microwave until it's easy to roll (but not so hot that it hardens or turns brown).

3. Spoon the heated tofu mixture onto the middle of the tortilla. Add the guacamole or avocado, pico de gallo, and any optional add-ins. Assemble the contents on the tortilla in a lengthwise manner, so you have two large flaps of bare tortilla on either side and small flaps of tortilla on the top and bottom.

4. To fold your burrito, fold the small flaps at the top and bottom over the contents and then fold the large flaps over. Seal it shut with a small bit of guacamole (or mashed avocado). Wrap the burrito with aluminum foil to keep it warm and to hold it together as you're eating it.

My Tips

Waffles

I often make these waffles when I have friends over for brunch, and now some even request them specifically when they come to town. I set out a waffle topping bar with pure maple syrup (a must), fresh seasonal berries, vegan yogurt or whipped cream, coconut shreds, strawberry preserves, and whatever else I have on hand so everyone can customize their waffle to their liking.

Yield: 4–6 waffles

Prep time: 10 minutes | Cook time: 20 minutes | Total time: 30 minutes

You'll need: a waffle iron

2 cups plant-based milk (any variety)
2 tablespoons ground flaxseed meal
¼ cup canola oil
1 teaspoon vanilla extract
2 cups all-purpose flour
1 tablespoon baking powder
2 tablespoons granulated sugar
¼ teaspoon salt
½ cup vegan chocolate chips (optional)
Pure maple syrup, to taste
Strawberry preserves (store-bought or from the recipe on page 245)

1. Turn on a waffle iron.
2. In a medium bowl, whisk together the plant-based milk, flaxseed meal, canola oil, and vanilla extract. Set aside.
3. In a large bowl, whisk together the flour, baking powder, sugar, and salt.
4. Create a well in the center of the dry ingredients and pour in the milk mixture. Whisk gently, just until combined (some clumps are fine and will dissolve on their own). Add the chocolate chips (if using) and mix them in gently. Do not overmix.
5. Scoop the desired amount of batter onto the preheated waffle iron. Follow your waffle iron instructions to cook. Repeat with the remaining batter until all the waffles are cooked.
6. Top with maple syrup, strawberry preserves, and any additional toppings you like.

Love Your Leftovers: Have extra batter? You can store it in the fridge for several days and cook up fresh waffles whenever you want them. Or, if you made extra waffles, you can freeze them, then pop them in the toaster oven whenever you want a quick, no-fuss breakfast.

My Tips

Toaster Pastries

When we were growing up, Pop-Tarts were a vending machine favorite of ours. Little did we know, most contain gelatin (which comes from animal skin and bones) and therefore aren't even vegetarian! Whether you were a lover or hater of those old-school pastries, *these* DIY pastries will totally blow your mind. They are decadent, buttery, and the perfect mix of fruity and sweet. We recommend making these on a day when you're not pressed for time so you can really enjoy the process and have fun with it.

Yield: 10–12 toaster pastries

Prep time: 45 minutes | Cook time: 30 minutes | Total time: 2 hours and 15 minutes

You'll need: a food processor

4 cups all-purpose flour
4 teaspoons granulated sugar
1½ cups chilled vegan butter, chopped into chunks
6 tablespoons cold water, plus additional as needed
1½ cups jam or preserves
2 cups powdered sugar
¼ cup vanilla soy milk (sweetened or unsweetened)
Vegan rainbow sprinkles (or your favorite decorative toppings)

1. Place the flour, sugar, and cold butter chunks in the bowl of a food processor. Pulse minimally until the butter is mostly incorporated and a loose, crumbly powder forms.

2. Add 6 tablespoons of water to the food processor and pulse again until clumps begin to form. If the clumps can be hand-formed into a dough at this point, move to step 3. If the mixture is too crumbly to form into a dough, more liquid is needed—add additional cold water 1 tablespoon at a time just until you can hand-form the clumps into a dough.

3. Form the dough into a rectangular patty, wrap it tightly in plastic wrap, and refrigerate for at least 1 hour.

4. Preheat the oven to 350 degrees F. Line a baking sheet with parchment paper or a silicone mat.

5. Remove the dough from the fridge. Unwrap it and place on a large lightly floured surface or countertop. Using a floured rolling pin, gently roll the dough out to a ⅛-inch thickness, or as thinly as possible without breaking it. The total size should be at least 12½ × 16 inches. (If your

work surface is not large enough, split the dough into two parts before rolling it out and refrigerate the second part until ready to use.) Once the dough is rolled into a thin sheet, use a pizza cutter or sharp knife to cut out 2½ × 4-inch rectangles of dough. While rolling, press together broken edges of dough as needed to fit as many rectangles as possible. You should be able to get 20 to 24 rectangles out of the dough.

6. Using a thin spatula, place half of the dough rectangles on the prepared baking sheet. Fit as many as you can, leaving ½ inch between each slice. Add 1 to 2 tablespoons of jam along the center of each dough slice. Place an additional dough slice on top of each jam-covered slice and seal all four edges using a fork, gently pressing down the fork prongs into both layers of dough. If the dough doesn't seem completely sealed, it's okay. There is no harm if some jam seeps out during baking. Using a toothpick, pierce three or four holes on the top of each pastry. Repeat until you've used up all your dough.

7. Bake the pastries for 25 to 30 minutes, until very lightly golden around the edges. Remove from the oven and allow to cool for a few minutes on the baking sheet. Using a spatula, transfer the pastries to a cooling rack to completely cool before icing.

8. To prepare the icing, pour the powdered sugar and vanilla soy milk into a small bowl and whisk until combined. The icing should be thick so that the majority will stay atop the pastry.

9. Place a paper towel or parchment paper below the cooling rack to catch icing drips. Spoon the icing onto the middle of the cooled tarts, nudging it outward and allowing some to naturally drip off the sides. Add the sprinkles before the icing dries and hardens.

Friendly Suggestion: You can fill these with the jelly or jam of your choice—but if you want to get really fancy, make your own three-ingredient Strawberry Preserves (page 245).

My Tips

_____

_____

_____

Pancakes

A golden stack of these fluffy pancakes will impress your brunch buddies and have them asking for your recipe. Add a handful of blueberries or chocolate chips to the batter for texture and flavor, and load up on toppings like maple syrup, fruit, whipped cream, coconut shreds, or even a drizzle of warmed peanut butter.

Yield: 4–6 servings

Prep time: 10 minutes | Cook time: 20 minutes | Total time: 30 minutes

1 tablespoon ground flaxseed meal

3 tablespoons warm water

1½ cups all-purpose flour

1 tablespoon baking powder

¼ teaspoon salt

3 tablespoons granulated sugar

1½ cups plant-based milk (any variety)

3 tablespoons vegan butter

2 teaspoons vanilla extract

Vegetable oil (or spray), for frying

Optional Toppings:

Pure maple syrup

Fresh fruit

1. In a small bowl, beat together the flaxseed meal and water for 1 minute. Set aside for 5 minutes to let the mixture thicken.

2. In a large bowl, sift together the flour, baking powder, salt, and sugar.

3. Place the plant-based milk and vegan butter in a medium microwave-safe bowl, and microwave for 1 minute and 30 seconds or until the butter is completely melted. Add the butter mixture, vanilla extract, and flaxseed meal mixture to the dry mixture and gently whisk by hand just until the batter is smooth, but there's no need to remove all the lumps. Do not overmix.

4. Heat a small amount of vegetable oil in a large nonstick pan over medium heat. It's important for the pan to preheat before making your first pancake.

5. With a ½-cup measuring cup, scoop up some batter and pour it onto the preheated pan, using the cup to spread the batter and shape each pancake to the size you like. Once lots of bubbles begin to form on the pancakes, in 2 to 3 minutes, flip the pancakes over and cook the other side until light brown.

(Continues)

6. Remove the cooked pancakes from the heat. (To keep the pancakes warm while you're cooking, you can place the finished ones on a baking sheet in a warm oven set at 200 degrees F.) Repeat step 5 with the remaining batter, until all the batter is cooked.

7. Serve immediately and top with any optional toppings.

My Tips

Jen's Cinnamon Rolls

Nothing beats the comforting smell of warm cinnamon buns baking in the oven. Our friend Jen Regan would make these every Friday morning at her all-vegan Poison Berry Bakery in Cleveland, Ohio, and her regular customers came in like clockwork to stock up, calling them "magical" and "life changing." Sadly for us, Jen has since moved on to other adventures, but we're excited to help these cinnamon rolls live on in homes all around the world with Jen's recipe.

Yield: 12 rolls

Prep time: 45 minutes | Cook time: 20 minutes | Total time: 3 hours and 13 minutes

You'll need: an electric hand mixer

Dough:

2 tablespoons ground flaxseed meal

5 tablespoons plus ¼ cup warm water, divided

¾ cup soy milk (any variety)

¼ cup vegan butter

1½ tablespoons active dry yeast

¼ cup granulated sugar, divided

1 teaspoon vanilla extract

3¼ cups all-purpose flour, divided

½ teaspoon salt

Filling:

½ cup vegan butter, softened at room temperature

1 cup packed brown sugar

1½ tablespoons ground cinnamon

Frosting:

½ (8-ounce) container plain vegan cream cheese (we recommend the brand Tofutti)

¼ cup vegan butter, softened at room temperature

1½ cups powdered sugar

½ teaspoon vanilla extract, plus additional if needed to thin out

Pinch of salt

1. To make the dough, in a small bowl, whisk together the flaxseed meal and 5 tablespoons of warm water. Set aside to rest and thicken for at least 5 minutes.

2. In a medium pot over medium heat, heat the soy milk until tiny bubbles form. Remove from the heat, stir in the vegan butter, and let cool to room temperature.

3. In a large bowl, mix together the yeast, 1 teaspoon of the granulated sugar, and ¼ cup of warm water. Let the mixture sit for 10 minutes to activate the yeast. Add the flaxseed meal mixture, soy milk mixture, and vanilla extract. Using a

fork, stir in 2¼ cups of the flour, the remaining granulated sugar (¼ cup minus 1 teaspoon), and the salt.

4. Gradually add the remaining 1 cup of flour and knead for about 5 minutes, until the flour is incorporated and the dough is smooth. Form the dough into a ball in the bowl, cover with a damp paper towel, and let rise for 1 hour in a warm place (ideally 80 to 90 degrees F).

5. To make the filling, in a small bowl, combine the vegan butter, brown sugar, and cinnamon and mash with a fork until the butter is fully incorporated and no chunks remain. Set aside.

6. On a floured surface, using a floured rolling pin, roll out the dough into a 12 × 15-inch rectangle. Using your fingers, spread the brown sugar mixture evenly across the dough. Starting at one of the shorter sides, tightly roll the dough so you have a 12-inch-long roll. Pinch to seal. With a sharp knife, cut the roll into 12 equally sized slices and place them on a baking sheet lined with parchment paper or a silicone mat. Cover with a damp towel or paper towel and let rise for 1 to 2 hours, until doubled in size.

7. Preheat the oven to 350 degrees F. Bake the rolls for 20 minutes or until they are golden brown and a toothpick inserted in the center comes out clean. Do not overbake.

8. Using a spatula, lift the rolls off the pan immediately to prevent the filling from sticking, and transfer to a cooling rack. Allow the rolls to cool fully before frosting.

9. To prepare the frosting, using an electric hand mixer, beat together the vegan cream cheese and butter in a medium bowl. Add the powdered sugar, vanilla extract, and salt and beat until the frosting is smooth and thick. Spread the frosting evenly over each cinnamon bun.

My Tips

Challah French Toast

Challah (page 257) is best enjoyed fresh, torn from the loaf straight out of the oven, but don't let that day-old (or two-day-old) challah go to waste! Even after it gets a little too hard to enjoy on its own, it makes the *perfect* base for French toast. This is a denser, chewier spin on traditional French toast and is a classic weekend breakfast in many Jewish households. Michelle has many fond childhood memories of waking up to the sweet, cinnamony smell of challah French toast cooking in the kitchen, and we both plan to continue this tradition. We hope you'll do the same.

Yield: 6–8 servings

Prep time: 40 minutes | Cook time: 40 minutes | Total time: 3 hours and 45 minutes

You'll need: a blender

1 loaf vegan challah (store-bought or from the recipe on page 257)
1 (14-ounce) block silken (also called "soft") tofu, drained
¼ cup unsweetened, plain soy milk
1 teaspoon ground flaxseed meal

1 teaspoon vanilla extract
1 teaspoon cornstarch
1½ tablespoons all-purpose flour
2 tablespoons granulated sugar
1 teaspoon ground cinnamon
⅛ teaspoon salt

2 tablespoons canola oil, plus additional as needed

Optional Toppings:

Maple syrup
Powdered sugar
Vegan butter
Fresh fruit
Vegan whipped cream

1. If you're using fresh challah, preheat the oven (or toaster oven) to 300 degrees F. Slice the challah into ¾-inch-thick slices, arrange them on a baking sheet, and bake for 10 minutes. If you're using challah that's a few days old and already dried out, skip this step.

2. In a blender, purée the tofu, soy milk, flaxseed meal, and vanilla extract. Allow the mixture to sit for 5 minutes. Then add the cornstarch, flour, sugar, cinnamon, and salt and blend again until smooth. Pour the batter into a bowl large enough to easily dip the bread in.

3. Heat 1 tablespoon of canola oil in a large nonstick skillet over medium heat. Working with a few slices at a time, dip challah slices into the batter, allowing each side to bathe in the batter for 20 to 40 seconds, and place on the pan. Cook for about 5 minutes on each side, until lightly browned, and then, using a spatula and the side of the pan, gently lift the bread to rest on its sides to lightly cook those portions. It's okay if there are some little batter areas that

don't hit the pan. Repeat with the remaining slices, adding more oil to the pan as needed.

4. Serve immediately with any optional toppings.

My Tips

_____

_____

_____

Banana Bread

This is a veganized version of my grandmother's recipe, which has been passed down through the generations. It's one of the most memorable treats my dad would make while I was growing up, and I'm excited to pass this tradition on to you. This decadent, cakelike banana bread is not only insanely delicious, but also a great way to rescue bananas that are past their prime. In fact, the closer your bananas are to completely brown, the better they'll be for this recipe.

Yield: 1 loaf

Prep time: 15 minutes | Cook time: 1 hour | Total time: 1 hour and 15 minutes

You'll need: an electric mixer

2 tablespoons ground flaxseed meal

¼ cup plus 1 tablespoon water

½ cup vegetable shortening (such as Crisco)

¾ cup granulated sugar

1 teaspoon vanilla extract

2 cups all-purpose flour

1 teaspoon baking soda

¼ teaspoon salt

3 large, super-spotty, overripe bananas

⅓ cup vegan chocolate chips

1. Preheat the oven to 350 degrees F. Grease a standard 8½ × 4½-inch loaf pan.
2. In a small ramekin, mix together the flaxseed meal and water. Set aside for at least 5 minutes to allow the mixture to rest and thicken.
3. In a large bowl, beat together the shortening and sugar using an electric mixer until light and fluffy.
4. Add the flaxseed meal mixture and vanilla extract to the bowl and beat well.
5. In a separate, medium bowl, sift together the flour, baking soda, and salt. Add the flour mixture to the sugar mixture and beat until combined.
6. Add the bananas and chocolate chips, mashing the bananas and mixing everything together until well combined.
7. Pour the batter into the prepared loaf pan and bake for 50 to 60 minutes, until a toothpick dipped into the center of the bread comes out clean (aside from any melted chocolate). The top of the bread should be lightly browned.

Friendly Suggestion: If you love nuts, walnuts work well in this recipe. You may add ⅓ cup of chopped walnuts in step 6 without otherwise adjusting the recipe.

My Tips

_____

_____

_____

_____

_____

_____

_____

Blueberry Muffins

Muffins are a versatile treat that can be eaten for breakfast, a snack, or even dessert. Our recipe calls for fresh blueberries, but you can get creative and swap in apple chunks and add cinnamon, or walnuts and dried cranberries. The possibilities are as endless as your imagination!

Yield: 9 muffins

Prep time: 20 minutes | Cook time: 37 minutes | Total time: 57 minutes

1 tablespoon ground flaxseed meal
3 tablespoons warm water
1½ cups all-purpose flour
¾ cup granulated sugar
½ teaspoon salt
2 teaspoons baking powder
⅓ cup vegetable oil
⅓ cup soy milk (any variety)
1½ teaspoons vanilla extract
1¼ cups fresh blueberries, divided

1. Preheat the oven to 400 degrees F. Line a muffin pan with 9 paper or silicone liners.
2. In a small bowl, whisk together the flaxseed meal and warm water. Set aside for at least 5 minutes to allow the mixture to thicken.
3. In a large bowl, combine the flour, sugar, salt, and baking powder and mix well. Form a well in the middle of the dry ingredients and add the vegetable oil, flax meal mixture, soy milk, and vanilla extract. Gently mix together. Fold in 1 cup of the blueberries, reserving the rest for topping.
4. Pour the batter into the prepared muffin pan, filling each cup to the top. You should have enough for 9 muffins. Top with the remaining ¼ cup of blueberries, pushing them gently into the top of the batter.
5. Bake for about 37 minutes, until the muffins are golden on top and a toothpick inserted into the center of a muffin comes out clean.

Why It Works: Using fresh blueberries instead of frozen prevents your batter from turning blue. If you use frozen, your muffins will still taste delicious, but they will have a blue tint.

My Tips

_____

_____

Homemade Granola

This granola is delicious eaten on its own, served as a cereal with plant-based milk, or sprinkled atop yogurt, ice cream, or our Chia Pudding Parfait (page 203). In this recipe we've included our personal favorite combination of fruit, seeds, and nuts. The ground flaxseed meal helps everything bind together and also provides a nutritious boost of healthy omega-3s.

Yield: 6–8 servings

Prep time: 15 minutes | Cook time: 22 minutes | Total time: 1 hour and 37 minutes

3½ cups old-fashioned rolled oats

½ cup chopped raw walnuts

½ cup slivered raw almonds

½ cup raw pumpkin seeds (without shells)

1 tablespoon ground flaxseed meal

¾ teaspoon salt

½ teaspoon ground cinnamon

¼ cup packed brown sugar

¼ cup vegetable oil

¼ cup plus 1 tablespoon maple syrup

¾ cup raisins

1. Preheat the oven to 350 degrees F. Line a baking sheet with parchment paper or a silicone mat.

2. In a large bowl, combine the rolled oats, walnuts, almonds, pumpkin seeds, flaxseed meal, salt, cinnamon, and brown sugar. Pour in the vegetable oil and maple syrup and mix thoroughly until all the ingredients are evenly coated.

3. Pour the granola mix onto the prepared baking sheet and pat it down with a large spoon into an even layer. Bake for 22 minutes until golden brown.

4. Remove the granola from the oven, evenly sprinkle the raisins on top (don't stir), and allow to completely cool for 1 hour. Once the granola is completely cooled, mix it and store in an airtight container.

Tester Tip: "My family loves adding additional mix-ins to this granola. We add peanut butter sometimes, vegan chocolate chips, shredded coconut, dried fruit, and assorted nuts and seeds right to the mix before baking, depending on our taste that day." —Kim P.

My Tips

Chewy Chocolate Peanut Butter Granola Bars

We designed these bars after the ones we lusted after as kids. Chewy granola bars coated in chocolate were *obviously* the best, so we dip these in a rich chocolate that hardens when chilled and helps hold the bars together. Don't let this recipe intimidate you; these bars are super easy to prepare. Just make sure you use extra-ripe, soft, squishy Medjool dates. Dates that have been sitting on shelves for a long time won't work, because when desiccated and hard, they won't provide enough sticky adhesive power to hold these bars together.

Yield: 6–8 servings

Prep time: 20 minutes | Total time: 1 hour

You'll need: a food processor

Granola Bars:

- ½ cup creamy peanut butter (the kind with no oil separation), plus up to 3 tablespoons more as needed
- 1 tablespoon coconut oil (refined or unrefined)
- ⅔ cup tightly packed pitted Medjool dates (about 8 large dates)
- 1 tablespoon agave
- ¼ teaspoon vanilla extract
- ¼ teaspoon salt
- 1½ cups old-fashioned rolled oats
- ½ cup crisped rice cereal (such as Rice Krispies)

Chocolate Coating:

- ⅓ cup vegan chocolate chips
- ½ teaspoon coconut oil (refined or unrefined)

1. To make the granola bars, in a small microwave-safe ramekin, heat the peanut butter and coconut oil in the microwave for 30 seconds.

2. Spoon the warm peanut butter mixture into the bowl of a food processor and add the Medjool dates, agave, vanilla extract, salt, rolled oats, and crisped rice cereal. Pulse until fully combined but still chunky. The resulting mixture should be crumbly but able to stick together when pressed with your fingers. If the mixture is too dry to stick together, add up to 3 additional tablespoons of peanut butter, 1 tablespoon at a time, as needed.

3. Press the crumbly mixture into a medium container or small baking dish (9 × 7 inches is ideal) lined with parchment paper. Cover with another sheet of parchment paper and, using your hands, press the granola mixture into a square or rectangle that you'll be able to slice into bars. Push down very firmly across the entire patty to shape and ensure that the mixture sticks and stays together. Refrigerate for 20 minutes.

4. Just before you pull the granola out of the refrigerator, prepare your chocolate coating. In a small microwave-safe ramekin, melt the chocolate chips and coconut oil in the microwave, heating in 20-second increments and stirring between each until fully melted. (Microwaving for longer than 20 seconds at a time can destroy the chocolate.) Alternatively, you can melt the chocolate and coconut oil in a double boiler on the stove (see the box on page 19). You should have a silky-smooth melted chocolate mixture before moving to step 5.

5. Remove the chilled patty from the refrigerator and coat with the chocolate, using a small spatula or the back of a large spoon to spread. Allow the chocolate to harden slightly (about 30 minutes). Remove the patty from the baking dish and use a sharp chef's knife to slice into bars. You can make them thick or skinny, long or short, and can make as many as you'd like—it's up to you!

6. Place the bars on a dish or in a container and refrigerate until the chocolate has fully hardened.

7. Store the bars in the refrigerator until you're ready to enjoy.

Meal Prepping Tip: If you fall in love with these bars as much as we have, double the batch and freeze some so you don't have to make them as often. They freeze beautifully after the chocolate has hardened in the fridge.

My Tips

Instant Oatmeal Three Ways

As kids, we loved those little packets of instant oatmeal we would eat before running off to school. Today, we're more aware of both the cost and the environmental impact of prepackaged foods, which is how these three recipes were born. Michelle's favorite was always the strawberries and cream flavor, and Toni's was apple cinnamon. And of course, we can't forget the classic maple and brown sugar!

Strawberries & Cream Instant Oatmeal

Yield: 1 serving

Prep time: 5 minutes | Cook time: 1 minute and 30 seconds | Total time: 6 minutes and 30 seconds

⅓ cup instant oats
2½ teaspoons powdered sugar
⅛ teaspoon vanilla extract
2 tablespoons diced and crushed freeze-dried strawberries
½ cup unsweetened, plain soy milk

1. In a single-serving microwave-safe bowl, combine all the ingredients.
2. Microwave for 1 minute and 30 seconds. Serve warm.

Friendly Suggestion: This recipe also tastes delicious with fresh diced strawberries in place of freeze-dried.

My Tips

Apple Cinnamon Instant Oatmeal

Yield: 1 serving

Prep time: 5 minutes | Cook time: 1 minute and 30 seconds | Total time: 6 minutes and 30 seconds

⅓ cup instant oats

2½ teaspoons granulated sugar

⅛ teaspoon ground cinnamon

2 tablespoons finely diced freeze-dried apples

½ cup unsweetened, plain plant-based milk

1. In a single-serving microwave-safe bowl, combine all the ingredients. Mix well until no cinnamon clumps remain.
2. Microwave for 1 minute and 30 seconds. Serve warm.

Friendly Suggestion: This recipe is also delicious with finely diced Granny Smith apple (with peel removed) in place of the dried apple.

Maple & Brown Sugar Instant Oatmeal

Yield: 1 serving

Prep time: 5 minutes | Cook time: 1 minute and 30 seconds | Total time: 6 minutes and 30 seconds

⅓ cup instant oats

1½ teaspoons packed dark brown sugar

1 teaspoon pure maple syrup

½ cup unsweetened, plain plant-based milk

Pinch of salt

1. In a single-serving microwave-safe bowl, combine all the ingredients.
2. Microwave for 1 minute and 30 seconds. Serve warm.

Friendly Suggestion: If you want to save time, you can preassemble little glass jars with the dry ingredients so they're all ready—just pour them into a bowl, add your plant-based milk, and microwave for an easy breakfast in the morning.

Overnight Oats

This is the ultimate lazy vegan breakfast. With just three minutes of prep in the evening, breakfast will be waiting for you to grab and go in the morning. The uncooked oats will soak up the milk overnight and essentially "cook" themselves. This breakfast is meant to be enjoyed cold, but feel free to briefly pop it in the microwave if you prefer it warm. We encourage you to add an extra splash of milk or toppings before you dig in.

Yield: 1–2 servings

Prep time: 5 minutes | Total time: 5 minutes

1 cup old-fashioned rolled oats

1 cup plus 2–3 tablespoons plant-based milk (any variety), divided

½ cup blueberries (fresh or frozen)

1 tablespoon pure maple syrup

1 teaspoon vanilla extract

Optional Add-Ins:

1 tablespoon peanut butter (any type)

Sliced bananas

Ground cinnamon, to taste

1 teaspoon chia seeds

1. In a container, cup, or glass jar, combine the rolled oats, 1 cup of the plant-based milk, the blueberries, maple syrup, vanilla extract, and any optional add-ins. Mix well.

2. Cover and refrigerate overnight or for at least 3 hours.

3. Remove from the refrigerator, top with the remaining 2 to 3 tablespoons of plant-based milk and any optional additions, and enjoy chilled.

My Tips

Mango Smoothie

The simplicity of this three-ingredient smoothie is also the beauty of it. Mangoes are naturally sweet, and when frozen, they thicken up smoothies beautifully (especially when combined with fresh banana), giving a shake-like texture and flavor without the bad stuff. On busy mornings, you'll really appreciate how quickly and easily this comes together. You might be tempted to toss other fruit into the smoothie, but please give this a try exactly as is. The mingling of the mango and banana is what makes it so special.

Yield: 1 large smoothie or 2 small smoothies

Prep time: 5 minutes | Total time: 5 minutes

You'll need: a high-powered blender

2 cups frozen mango
1 ripe banana (not frozen)
1 cup unsweetened, plain soy milk (or any plant-based milk)

In a high-powered blender, blend all the ingredients until thick and creamy. There should be no clumps remaining—the smoothie should be a thick, creamy, magical mango delight. Enjoy immediately!

Friendly Suggestion: This smoothie is best enjoyed through a straw—but skip those planet-damaging plastic straws, please! Reach for a reusable glass or stainless steel straw instead. You can learn more about our favorite reusable straws and other eco-friendly products at FriendlyVeganCookbook.com.

My Tips

_____

_____

_____

Dinner & Entrées

This, our dear friends, is the heart of our cookbook. What to eat for dinner is a question we *all* ponder every day. Whether you're brand-new to vegan eating or a longtime herbivore itching for culinary inspiration, these recipes promise to nourish you while tantalizing your taste buds.

If you, like us, are a pasta lover, head straight to the Mac 'n' Cheese (page 63), Fettuccine Alfredo (page 75), and Pesto Pasta (page 81) recipes. The Chickpea "Tuna" Salad Sandwich (page 91) has been one of our lunchtime standards for years (you can also enjoy it as a wrap, a side, or just a snack), and Allison's Pot Pie (page 73)—though a little more labor-intensive than most of our recipes—is the ultimate comfort food dish.

One of the biggest challenges we face as plant-based eaters is gathering around food with friends, but there's nothing better than hearing your dinner guests say they can't believe their meal was vegan. Every recipe in this chapter was designed to elicit that response.

Lasagna

This flavorful lasagna is packed with tofu ricotta, spinach, and veggies, and makes a filling meal that will last for days. It's also an awesome dinner party meal and a comforting dish to bring to a friend who could use some TLC. You can even freeze pre-portioned cooked servings of this lasagna for an easy heat-and-enjoy meal.

Yield: 6–8 servings

Prep time: 30 minutes | Cook time: 45 minutes | Total time: 1 hour and 15 minutes

You'll need: a food processor

12 lasagna noodles (standard size, enough for 3 layers)
2 tablespoons olive oil
½ large yellow onion, diced
1 small zucchini, diced
1 cup sliced button mushrooms
4 large cloves garlic, roughly chopped
6 ounces fresh spinach
2 (16-ounce) blocks super-firm tofu, patted dry and cut into chunks for easy blending
¼ cup unsweetened, plain soy milk
2 tablespoons lemon juice
1 teaspoon dried basil or 1 tablespoon minced fresh basil leaves
2 teaspoons salt
5 cups marinara sauce (store-bought or from the recipe on page 228), divided
Fresh basil leaves, for garnish (optional)

1. In a large pot of boiling salted water, cook the lasagna noodles according to the directions on the package. Drain the noodles, rinse with cold water to cool, and set aside.

2. Heat the olive oil in a large skillet over medium heat. Add the onion, zucchini, mushrooms, and garlic and sauté for about 5 minutes, stirring occasionally, until slightly softened. Turn off the heat. Stir in the spinach, cover the skillet, and set aside to allow the spinach to wilt.

3. Place the tofu, soy milk, lemon juice, basil, and salt in the bowl of a food processor and pulse to combine. Depending on the size of your food processor, you may need to push everything down with a spoon several times between pulses so all the tofu gets evenly crumbled. When you reach a crumbly ricotta-style consistency, spoon the mixture into a large bowl. Stir in the sautéed vegetables and spinach until evenly combined.

4. Preheat the oven to 350 degrees F.

5. Spread 1 cup of the marinara sauce evenly across the bottom of a 9 × 13-inch baking dish. Follow this with a layer of 4 overlapping lasagna noodles, then a layer of half of the tofu mixture. Repeat with another 1½ cups of the marinara, another

layer of noodles, and the second half of the tofu mixture. End with another 1½ cups of the marinara and a final layer of noodles, and spread the remaining 1 cup of marinara sauce on top, being sure to coat all the noodles.

6. Bake for 45 minutes. Garnish with the basil leaves (if using).

Meal Prepping Tip: You can prepare this lasagna in advance and keep it in the refrigerator (or freezer!) until you're ready to bake it. If the lasagna is frozen, thaw in the refrigerator for 24 hours before baking. If you bake it from a refrigerated state, increase the bake time to 1 hour or until heated all the way through.

My Tips

Mac 'n' Cheese

We're a little obsessed with mac 'n' cheese. We've tried every packaged vegan version we could get our paws on over the past decade, and we've made dozens of varieties from scratch. This is the best of them all—a creamy, decadent mac 'n' cheese that will have your friends begging for the recipe. This mac makes a great party dish, and we served it at Michelle's baby shower, Toni's housewarming, and many other family gatherings.

Yield: 6–8 servings

Prep time: 25 minutes | Cook time: 21 minutes | Total time: 46 minutes

1 (16-ounce) package macaroni (or your favorite pasta)
½ cup vegan butter
½ medium yellow onion, diced
½ cup all-purpose flour
2 teaspoons salt
2 tablespoons soy sauce
3 medium cloves garlic, minced
¾ teaspoon ground turmeric
1 cup nutritional yeast
½ teaspoon ground black pepper
½ teaspoon red chili pepper flakes (optional)
1 head broccoli, cut into small florets and steamed
½ cup vegan cheese shreds (optional)
½ cup panko bread crumbs
½ teaspoon paprika

1. In a large pot of boiling water, cook the pasta according to the directions on the package. Drain the cooked pasta over a bowl to retain the pasta water and set aside.
2. Preheat the oven to 350 degrees F.
3. In a large pot over medium heat, melt the vegan butter. Add the onion and sauté until it becomes translucent, about 5 minutes. Whisk in the flour and stir until the mixture thickens and becomes a roux, 3 to 5 minutes.
4. Whisk 3½ cups of the reserved pasta water into the roux. Add the salt, soy sauce, garlic, turmeric, nutritional yeast, black pepper, and red chili pepper flakes (if using), and stir until the sauce thickens.
5. Stir the cooked pasta and steamed broccoli florets into the cheese sauce. Transfer the cheesy pasta into a 9 × 13-inch casserole dish. Top the pasta with the vegan cheese shreds (if using) and panko bread crumbs, and sprinkle with the paprika.
6. Bake for 20 minutes.
7. Turn the oven heat to broil, and broil for about 1 minute, until the top gets slightly crispy and lightly browned.

Meal Prepping Tips: If you're preparing this mac for an event, you can make it ahead of time and refrigerate it after step 5. Pull it out to bake when you're ready to party. You can also bake it and refrigerate your leftovers. This is a phenomenal bake-and-save casserole that's as delicious on day five as it is fresh out of the oven.

My Tips

Yellow Tofu Curry

We love Thai curry. And since we're huge potato lovers, we always go for yellow curry with tofu when we go out to a Thai restaurant. This homemade curry is just as good as the kind you'd find while dining out. This recipe does require a specialty ingredient—yellow curry paste, which you can find at many grocery stores. But if you have trouble finding it locally, you can also order it online.

Yield: 4–6 servings

Prep time: 20 minutes | Cook time: 30 minutes | Total time: 50 minutes

1 tablespoon vegetable oil

1 small yellow onion, sliced

1 large red bell pepper, sliced

2 carrots, sliced

2 large Yukon Gold potatoes (about 1 pound), cut into 1-inch bite-sized pieces

⅓ cup yellow curry paste

2 (13.5-ounce) cans full-fat coconut milk

1 tablespoon packed brown sugar

1 teaspoon salt

1 teaspoon red chili pepper flakes (adjust according to your spice preference)

2 cups bite-sized broccoli pieces

1 (16-ounce) block extra-firm tofu, drained and cut into bite-sized cubes

4–6 cups cooked white or brown rice

1. Heat the vegetable oil in a large pot over medium-high heat. Add the onion, bell pepper, and carrots, and sauté for 2 to 3 minutes, until the bell pepper is tender.

2. Add the potatoes and curry paste and sauté for another 3 to 4 minutes.

3. Pour in the coconut milk, and stir in the brown sugar, salt, and red chili pepper flakes.

4. Bring to a boil and cover. Lower the heat and simmer for 15 minutes. Add the broccoli and tofu and continue simmering, covered, for 15 more minutes.

5. Serve with the rice.

Friendly Suggestion: If you like your tofu to be very firm, sauté it in 1 tablespoon of canola oil for 3 to 4 minutes before adding it in step 4.

> **My Tips**
> _____
> _____
> _____

Shepherd's Pie

You're going to love this flavorful, decadent meal that smells like Thanksgiving. It was inspired by a recipe from our Plant-Based on a Budget Meal Plans (which you can find over at Plant-BasedMealPlan.com). Traditional shepherd's pie calls for lamb meat, but don't worry, friends. No sweet, fluffy sheep will be sacrificed for this delicious comfort meal. Instead, we're turning to a healthful, versatile, ultra-affordable legume: the lentil.

Yield: 6–8 servings

Prep time: 15 minutes | Cook time: 35 minutes | Total time: 50 minutes

1 tablespoon vegetable oil
1 carrot, finely diced
2 ribs celery, diced
½ medium yellow onion, diced
2 large cloves garlic, minced
1 cup chopped button mushrooms (optional)
1 cup dried brown lentils, rinsed and drained
1¾ cups vegetable broth (or equivalent amount of vegetable bouillon and water)
½ batch Mashed Potatoes (page 130)
Chopped parsley, for garnish (optional)
1 batch Mushroom Gravy (page 231)

1. Heat the vegetable oil in a large saucepan (with a lid) over medium heat. Add the carrot, celery, onion, garlic, and mushrooms (if using) and sauté, stirring occasionally, for 5 to 7 minutes, until the carrot is slightly softened.

2. Add the lentils and vegetable broth. Bring to a boil, cover, and then reduce the heat to a simmer. Simmer for 20 to 30 minutes, until the lentils are soft and all the liquid has been absorbed.

3. Preheat the oven to 400 degrees F.

4. Spread the lentil and vegetable mixture in a 9 × 13-inch baking dish and top with the mashed potatoes. Bake for 10 to 15 minutes, until the potatoes turn golden. You can also broil for 1 minute before taking it out of the oven to get it extra golden.

5. Top with parsley, if using, and serve with the mushroom gravy on top.

My Tips

Stuffed Shells

This dish is surprisingly easy to prepare and will make you feel like a top chef. It's also a showstopper that never fails to wow our dinner party guests. The flavor of the sauce is carried throughout the dish, so a great marinara (try page 228) or arrabbiata sauce is crucial!

Yield: 25+ stuffed shells (6–8 servings)

Prep time: 20 minutes | Cook time: 40 minutes | Total time: 1 hour

You'll need: a food processor

1 (12-ounce) package jumbo pasta shells
1 (16-ounce) block firm (or extra-firm) tofu, pressed
1 medium yellow onion, roughly chopped
5 medium cloves garlic
¼ cup packed fresh basil leaves
2 teaspoons dried oregano
2 teaspoons salt
¾ teaspoon ground black pepper
¼ teaspoon red chili pepper flakes (optional)
2 tablespoons nutritional yeast
Juice of 1 medium lemon
1 cup packed spinach leaves
1 (25-ounce) jar flavorful marinara sauce (or 1 batch of the recipe on page 228), divided
½ cup vegan cheese shreds (optional)
Fresh basil leaves, for garnish (optional)

1. In a large pot of boiling water, cook the jumbo pasta shells according to the prebake cooking directions on the package. Then drain, rinse with cold water to prevent sticking, and set aside.

2. Meanwhile, in the bowl of a food processor, combine the tofu, onion, garlic, basil, oregano, salt, black pepper, red chili pepper flakes (if using), nutritional yeast, and lemon juice. Pulse 15 times or until partially mixed. Add the spinach and pulse just a few more times until combined. The resulting texture should be ricotta-like. *Do not overpulse or your ricotta will turn green!*

3. Preheat the oven to 375 degrees F. Pour half of the marinara sauce into a 9 × 13-inch baking dish, spreading to evenly coat the bottom of the dish.

4. One by one, fill each cooked shell with a generous spoonful of the tofu ricotta filling and place in the prepared baking dish. Continue until the tofu mixture is gone and the baking dish is filled. Sprinkle the vegan cheese (if using) on top.

5. Drizzle the remaining marinara sauce over the stuffed shells. Cover the pan with aluminum foil and bake for 20 minutes. Remove the foil and bake for another 20 minutes or until the cheese (if using) is melted and the edges of the shells are lightly browned. Garnish with the basil leaves (if using). Serve immediately and enjoy hot.

Friendly Suggestion: You will likely have several cooked pasta shells left over, and they can be enjoyed just as you would any other pasta. We love dressing them with extra-virgin olive oil, garlic powder, salt, red chili pepper flakes, and nutritional yeast.

My Tips

_____

_____

Allison's Pot Pie

This pot pie is going to rock your world. It originates from our dear friend Allison Rivers Samson, who is a genius at magically transforming veggies into savory delights. This recipe takes a little more time to prepare, so pour yourself a favorite beverage, put on some tunes (or maybe an episode of *The Plant-Powered People Podcast*), and enjoy the process. The time you spend in the kitchen will be well worth it, and this one dish can provide you with many tasty meals throughout the entire week.

Yield: 8 servings

Prep time: 1 hour | Cook time: 45 minutes | Total time: 2 hours

You'll need: a food processor and a high-powered blender

Crust:

2¼ cups all-purpose flour
½ teaspoon salt
½ cup plus 2 tablespoons vegan butter
¼ cup ice water, plus up to 5 additional tablespoons as needed to form a dough

Vegetable Filling:

2 tablespoons vegetable oil
3 cups diced yellow onions
2 cups sliced button mushrooms
1⅓ cups diced carrots
1 large clove garlic, minced
2 teaspoons salt
¾ teaspoon dried basil
¾ teaspoon dried marjoram
¾ teaspoon ground black pepper
8 ounces (half a 16-ounce block) extra-firm tofu, drained and sliced into tiny cubes
1 cup frozen green peas
2½ cups cubed yellow potatoes, steamed until soft

Béchamel Sauce:

3 cups water
¾ cup raw cashews
1½ teaspoons Dijon mustard
1 teaspoon salt
⅛ teaspoon ground nutmeg
¼ cup vegan butter
½ cup all-purpose flour

1. To prepare the crust, combine the flour, salt, and vegan butter in the bowl of a food processor and pulse until the mixture looks like a coarse meal. Add ¼ cup of ice water and pulse until the dough clumps together, but do not overmix. When you squeeze the clumps with your hand, the mixture should come together to form a pliable (but not moist or sticky) dough. If needed, add more water 1 tablespoon at a time until you reach that consistency. Between two sheets of parchment paper on a baking sheet, roll the dough to a 10 × 12-inch rectangle (about ¼ inch thick). Chill the rolled-out dough in the refrigerator (keep it on the baking sheet to make it easy to transfer) for at least 15 minutes.

2. To make the vegetable filling, heat the vegetable oil in a large sauté pan over medium heat. Add the onions and sauté for about 5 minutes, until the onions are translucent. Add the mushrooms, carrots, garlic, salt, basil, marjoram, and pepper and sauté for another 5 minutes. Remove the pan from the heat and fold in the tofu, peas, and potatoes. Set aside.

3. Preheat the oven to 450 degrees F.

4. To make the béchamel sauce, in a high-powered blender, combine the water, cashews, mustard, salt, and nutmeg and blend until completely smooth. In a medium saucepan over medium-low heat, melt the vegan butter and add the flour. Whisk for 2 minutes until the mixture begins to clump and toast up into a roux. Whisk in the cashew cream mixture. Increase the heat to medium and cook, whisking frequently, for about 10 minutes, until the sauce thickens.

5. Pour the sauce over the sautéed vegetables and stir to combine into a stew. Transfer to a 9 × 13-inch baking dish.

6. Remove the chilled crust from the refrigerator and peel off the top sheet of parchment. Lift the bottom sheet of parchment along with the dough and invert the dough onto the top of the stew. Slice 8 to 10 decorative 2-inch slits into the crust as vent holes.

7. Place the baking dish onto a rimmed baking sheet to catch any drips. Bake for 30 minutes. Turn on the broiler and broil for about 5 minutes to lightly brown the top. Serve hot.

Friendly Suggestion: No time to make your own piecrust? Frozen crusts work great with this recipe. You can also bake individual pot pies in small ramekins, topping with a round of crust and slicing an *X* in the center of each top to vent.

My Tips

Fettuccine Alfredo

Fettuccine Alfredo was one of my favorite dishes growing up, so I was eager to re-create and perfect it, vegan-style. This is just as decadent and creamy as the kind I grew up eating, and made entirely from plants! It's also made without a drop of butter. Most Alfredo recipes call for upward of half a cup of butter, which you'll see is *totally* unnecessary. This recipe is now a go-to in both of our homes and is an excellent dish to make when friends come over for dinner. And because it's all cooked in one pot, you'll have minimal cleanup at the end.

Yield: 6–8 servings

Prep time: 25 minutes | Cook time: 25 minutes | Total time: 55 minutes

You'll need: a high-powered blender and a nut milk bag

1 cup raw unsalted almonds

3 cups plus 2 tablespoons water, divided

1 tablespoon extra-virgin olive oil

1 medium yellow onion, diced

5 large cloves garlic, minced

4 cups low-sodium vegetable broth (or the equivalent amount of vegetable bouillon and water)

1 (16-ounce) package fettuccine

4 teaspoons cornstarch

1 tablespoon salt (only if using low-sodium broth)

1 teaspoon ground black pepper

Freshly cracked black pepper to taste, for garnish

½ cup finely chopped fresh parsley, for garnish

1. Using a high-powered blender, blend the almonds and 3 cups of water until a creamy milk forms. Over a large bowl, pour the liquid through a nut milk bag to strain out the pulp, and gently massage the bag until all the milk has passed through and only a thick crumbly clump of almond pulp remains. Set aside the silky-smooth almond cream and discard the pulp (or save it to use in another recipe).

2. Heat the olive oil in a large pot over medium heat. Add the onion and garlic and sauté for 2 to 4 minutes, until soft and fragrant.

3. Add the vegetable broth and homemade almond milk, increase the heat to medium-high, and bring to a boil.

4. Add the fettuccine to the pot and cook uncovered for the amount of time suggested on the package or until the noodles are cooked and tender. This will take 9 to 12 minutes, but can vary depending on the type of pasta you use. Stir the pasta frequently to prevent it from clumping and sticking to the bottom of the pan.

5. While the pasta is cooking, mix the cornstarch and 2 tablespoons of water in a small bowl until the cornstarch dissolves.
6. Two minutes before the pasta is done, add the cornstarch and water mixture, salt, and ground black pepper to the pot. Cook for 2 to 5 minutes, until the sauce starts to thicken.
7. Turn the heat off and allow the pasta and sauce to rest on the stove for 5 minutes to thicken. If the sauce is still very liquid, turn the heat on while mixing the pasta and sauce for another 1 to 2 minutes—but keep in mind that the sauce will continue to thicken with time.
8. Plate the pasta and garnish with the cracked black pepper and parsley.

Love Your Leftovers: Wondering what to do with the remaining fiber-rich almond meal from the almond cream you made? I usually pop it in my fridge and add it to my morning smoothies. You can also go to FriendlyVeganCookbook.com and find countless other recipes to use it in (cookies, muffins, and beyond).

My Tips

Ratatouille

This recipe is special not only because it's so beautiful, healthful, and full of Mediterranean flavors, but because it's a recipe from our cookbook food photographer, Zhoro Apostolov. This recipe is quite simple and highlights the natural beauty of seasonal produce. Be sure to use a well-seasoned marinara sauce (like ours on page 228), since the ratatouille's flavor is dependent on it!

Yield: 4–8 servings

Prep time: 45 minutes | Cook time: 40 minutes | Total time: 1 hour and 25 minutes

1 tablespoon extra-virgin olive oil
2 medium cloves garlic, minced
2 medium red onions, thinly sliced, divided
1 (25-ounce) jar flavorful marinara sauce (or 1 batch of the recipe on page 228)
Salt and pepper, to taste
1 sprig fresh thyme, plus additional for garnish
1 medium eggplant
1 medium zucchini
2 red bell peppers
2 Roma tomatoes
Lemon slices, for garnish (optional)

My Tips

1. Preheat the oven to 350 degrees F.
2. Make the sauce: Heat the olive oil in a saucepan over medium-high heat. Add the garlic and one-quarter of the onions and sauté for 2 minutes or until fragrant. Add the marinara sauce and season with salt and pepper. Let the sauce simmer for 3 to 4 minutes, then add the little leaves from the sprig of fresh thyme. This will be your base for the ratatouille.
3. Spread the sauce evenly on the bottom of a casserole dish or baking dish (around 8 × 8 inches in size).
4. Slice the eggplant, zucchini, bell peppers, and tomatoes very thin, about ¼ of an inch thick, or even thinner if desired. Make the slices consistent in size so they will bake evenly.
5. Arrange the sliced eggplant, zucchini, bell peppers, and tomatoes and the remaining sliced onions in alternating layers in the casserole dish. You can arrange them in circles (as shown in the photo), spirals, or straight lines depending on what fits better in your dish. Season with salt and pepper.
6. Bake for 30 to 40 minutes, until the vegetables are tender.
7. Garnish with thyme sprigs and lemon slices (if using).

Pesto Pasta

We are obsessed with our homemade Pesto (page 227), which is made with walnuts instead of pine nuts. Using walnuts instead of pine nuts will save you loads of money without compromising the flavor. Use any type of pasta you'd like—spaghetti, fettuccine, baby shells, macaroni—and serve this dish warm or cold. Want to make this even more nutritious? Toss in your favorite sautéed veggies (such as broccoli or red bell peppers) or some steamed kale. Any way you go, this is the perfect weeknight meal to throw together.

Yield: 4–6 servings

Prep: 15 minutes | Cook time: 15 minutes | Total time: 30 minutes

1 (16-ounce) package of
   your favorite pasta
1 batch Pesto (page 227)
Salt, to taste
1 tablespoon chopped
   walnuts, for garnish
   (optional)

1. In a large pot of boiling water, cook the pasta according to the directions on the package. Drain thoroughly.
2. Combine the pesto with the cooked noodles.
3. Serve with an extra sprinkle of salt and garnish with the chopped walnuts (if using).

My Tips

Cornbread Chili Casserole

Cornbread and chili is a comfort-food combo made in culinary heaven. Instead of chili with a *side* of cornbread, we put them together in one party-friendly casserole dish. When we have a crowd to feed, we make a double batch and watch it disappear in no time flat.

Yield: 8 servings

Prep time: 15 minutes | Cook time: 20 minutes | Total time: 35 minutes

1 batch Our Favorite Chili
(page 115)
1 batch Cornbread batter
(page 253; stop at
step 4)
Chopped fresh parsley,
for garnish (optional)

1. Preheat the oven to 425 degrees F.
2. Pour the chili into a 9 × 13-inch casserole dish and spread it out evenly. Remember to remove the bay leaf from the chili.
3. Using a spoon, dollop the cornbread batter onto the chili. It's okay if it doesn't completely cover the chili.
4. Bake for about 20 minutes, until the cornbread is lightly browned and a toothpick inserted into the center of the cornbread comes out clean.
5. Allow to cool for 15 minutes before serving.

My Tips

Beefy Tacos

If you follow us on social media, you know how much we love Taco Tuesday—and Taco Monday, Taco Thursday, and so on. We stuff these beauties with our own crumbled tofu "meat" and top with lettuce, avo, and classic pico de gallo salsa. If you're feeling tired of tacos (*gasp*), the meaty crumble works well in nachos and burritos, too. No food processor? Don't worry: this recipe will taste equally tacolicious if you crumble the tofu and chop the veggies by hand.

Yield: 8 tacos

Prep time: 20 minutes | Cook time: 20 minutes | Total time: 40 minutes

You'll need: a food processor

1 (16-ounce) block extra-firm tofu, drained and sliced into 1-inch cubes
¾ cup chopped red onion
½ red or green bell pepper, chopped
2 small cloves garlic
3½ tablespoons soy sauce
1 tablespoon ground cumin
1½ teaspoons chili powder
Pinch of smoked paprika
Pinch of salt
1 tablespoon vegetable oil
8 taco-sized corn or flour tortillas

Our Favorite Taco Toppings (Optional):

Pico de Gallo (page 242)
Chopped lettuce
Sliced avocado or guacamole
Lime wedges (serve on the side)

1. Preheat the oven to 375 degrees F. Lightly grease a baking sheet (or line it with parchment paper or a silicone mat).

2. Arrange the tofu in an even layer on the baking sheet and bake for 12 minutes. Allow the tofu to cool before proceeding.

3. In a food processor, combine the cooled tofu, onion, bell pepper, garlic, soy sauce, cumin, chili powder, paprika, and salt. Pulse a few times until the mixture forms into small crumbles.

4. In a large nonstick pan over high heat, heat the vegetable oil. Add the tofu mixture and cook, stirring frequently to prevent burning, for 8 to 10 minutes, until it begins to brown.

5. If you have a gas stove, turn the flame on medium-low on an empty burner and place the tortillas on top, one at a time, allowing them to toast directly on the flame. Flip the tortilla regularly (every 10 to 15 seconds) so it doesn't burn or catch fire. If you don't have a gas stove, toast your tortillas in a pan.

6. Lay the tortillas on a plate and spoon a generous serving of the tofu mixture onto each tortilla. Serve with any optional toppings.

Friendly Suggestion: Freezing your tofu overnight (or for at least 4 hours) and then thawing it before baking will create a chewy, extra-meaty texture.

Why It Works: Baking the tofu first pulls the moisture out and gives it a similar consistency to traditional taco meat. This step is essential (otherwise you'll have tofu mush when you put it in the food processor).

My Tips

My Tips

_____
_____
_____

Black Bean Burgers

Made with a base of black beans, brown rice, and sunflower seeds, this protein-packed burger is a healthy and satisfying alternative to store-bought vegan burgers. It's best cooked on a skillet (rather than a grill), but we kept the spirit of the outdoor dining experience alive by adding smoky-sweet barbecue sauce to the recipe.

Yield: 6 burgers

Prep time: 30 minutes | Cook time: 30 minutes | Total time: 1 hour

You'll need: a blender or food processor

1 cup raw unsalted sunflower seeds (no shells)
1 tablespoon chili powder
1½ tablespoons ground cumin
1 teaspoon smoked paprika
½ teaspoon salt
¼ teaspoon ground black pepper
1 tablespoon packed brown sugar

½ tablespoon olive oil, plus additional for cooking
½ medium yellow onion, finely diced
2 large cloves garlic, minced
1½ cups cooked black beans, drained, rinsed, and patted dry
1 cup cooked brown rice
⅓ cup panko bread crumbs

¼ cup vegan barbecue sauce (store-bought or from the recipe on page 237)

Burger Fixings:

Burger buns
Fresh greens
Sliced tomato
Sliced red onion
Sliced avocado
Vegan mayo or barbecue sauce

1. Heat a skillet over medium heat. Pour the sunflower seeds into the skillet and toast them, stirring frequently, for about 5 minutes, until they are golden brown. Allow to cool, and then tip them into a blender or food processor with the chili powder, cumin, paprika, salt, pepper, and brown sugar. Blend on high to create a coarse powder.
2. Heat the olive oil in a large skillet over medium-high heat. Add the onion and garlic, and sauté for 3 to 4 minutes, until the onion becomes translucent.
3. In a large bowl, mash the black beans using a potato masher or a fork.
4. Add everything else—the cooked rice, sunflower seed mixture, sautéed onion, panko bread crumbs, and barbecue sauce—to the bowl with the mashed beans. Mix until a pliable dough forms. Using your hands, press the dough into about six ¾-inch-thick patties.
5. Coat the skillet with olive oil and set it over medium heat. Add the burger patties and cook for 4 to 5 minutes on each side, until well browned.
6. Serve with your favorite burger fixings.

Jackfruit "Pulled Pork" Sandwich

Possibly the best way to enjoy our BBQ Pulled Jackfruit (page 232) is in a veganized pulled pork sandwich. Just grab a bun (or your favorite bread, toasted) and load it up with pulled jackfruit and your toppings of choice. We love adding shredded purple cabbage for crunch and color, plus red onion and tangy dill pickles. This also makes a tasty addition to a party platter (especially around football season). Just double or triple the batch of pulled jackfruit and get extra buns so there's enough to share, because it's guaranteed to be a hit.

Yield: 4 sandwiches

Prep time: 5 minutes | Total time: 5 minutes

1 batch BBQ Pulled Jackfruit (page 232)
1 cup finely shredded purple cabbage (or coleslaw, store-bought or from the recipe on page 162)
1 large red onion, finely sliced
Dill pickles, sliced, to taste
4 burger buns, toasted

Assemble each sandwich with a large scoop of hot BBQ pulled jackfruit topped with cabbage or coleslaw, red onion, and pickles on a toasted bun. Devour immediately.

Friendly Suggestion: Some brands of hamburger buns get soggy really easily. If that's a deal-breaker for you, try using a sturdier roll or ciabatta instead.

My Tips

Chickpea "Tuna" Salad Sandwich

 I've eaten about a thousand tuna salad sandwiches in my lifetime, and this is exactly how I used to make them in my pre-vegan days. Well, *almost* exactly. The biggest (and best) difference is that I swapped out the fish protein for one that is cheaper, more sustainable, and healthier. It might sound unbelievable that mashed chickpeas can take the place of fish, but trust us—it works! We often make this chickpea salad for nonvegan friends and family, who never fail to be amazed by its taste and texture. It was *made* for picnics and can be enjoyed in a sandwich, in a pita pocket, on crostini, over salad, in tuna melts, as a side, or served with crackers.

Yield: 4 sandwiches

Prep time: 20 minutes | Total time: 20 minutes

2 (15-ounce) cans chickpeas, rinsed and drained

¼ cup plus 1 tablespoon vegan mayo

½ tablespoon yellow mustard

½ cup finely diced red onion

½ cup diced celery

1 medium dill pickle, diced

¼ teaspoon salt

Ground black pepper, to taste

8 slices of your favorite bread

Toppings:

½ cup halved cherry tomatoes (optional)

Lettuce leaves

1. In a large bowl, mash the chickpeas with a potato masher or large fork.
2. Add the vegan mayo, mustard, onion, celery, pickle, salt, and pepper, and mix together thoroughly.
3. Scoop some of the chickpea salad onto a slice of bread. Top with cherry tomatoes (if using) and lettuce and press together with another piece of bread to make a sandwich. Repeat for the remaining sandwiches.

Tester Tip: "This is delicious wrapped in a large lettuce leaf." —Susan M.

My Tips

Sushi

Sushi making is extremely easy once you get the hang of it, and making it at home will save you *buckets* of money. Sushi at restaurants is *crazy* expensive, so instead of dining out, why not invite some friends over and have your own sushi night (or sushi-making party)? You'll come out of this experience with some special memories and very full, satisfied bellies.

   If this is your first time making sushi, we recommend watching a quick sushi mat tutorial online. Seeing the rolling process in action will help you get it right on the first try.

Yield: 5–6 servings

Prep time: 30 minutes | Cook time: 15 minutes | Total time: 1 hour

You'll need: a bamboo sushi mat

2 cups uncooked short-grain sushi rice
2⅓ cups water
2½ tablespoons rice vinegar
½ tablespoon granulated sugar
½ teaspoon salt
5–6 sheets sushi nori (toasted seaweed)
1 large avocado, pitted and sliced
1 carrot, sliced or shredded
1 small cucumber, cut into small strips

To serve:

Soy sauce
Wasabi
Pickled ginger

1. Place the rice in a large pot and fill with tap water to rinse. Using your hand, swish the rice around, drain, add more water, swish, and rinse again. Repeat this process a few times until the water stays mostly clear when swished. Drain the rinsing water.

2. Add 2⅓ cups of water to the rinsed rice in the large pot and mix. Bring to a boil over high heat. Stir the rice, lower the heat to medium-low, cover, and simmer for 15 minutes without removing the lid for any reason. Turn off the heat and wait an additional 10 minutes before removing the lid.

3. In a large bowl, combine the rice vinegar, sugar, and salt. Add the cooked rice while gently fluffing to mix. Set aside and allow the rice to cool to room temperature before using for sushi.

4. To assemble the sushi rolls, place one piece of nori (rough side up) in the center of the bamboo mat, and set a little bowl of water nearby to wet your fingers. With wet hands, spread a thin, even layer of room-temperature sushi rice across the entire sheet of seaweed (except the top ½ inch of

nori), pressing down gently as you spread. Add a small strip of avocado, carrot, and cucumber in a straight line about 1½ inches away from the bottom of the roll (nearest your hands). Using the bamboo mat, gently but tightly roll your sushi. Repeat with the remaining nori pieces until your rice is gone.

5. Using a sharp knife moistened with water, slice each roll into 6 to 8 pieces of sushi. Serve with soy sauce, wasabi, and pickled ginger.

Friendly Suggestion: Sushi rice should be used as soon as it's cool enough to work with. If you don't plan to use it right away, cover the top of your rice cooker or pot with a damp towel to prevent the rice from hardening.

My Tips

BLT Sandwich

A healthier version of a staple sandwich, this BLT is packed with all the salty-smoky flavor (and protein!) of the original, but without the cholesterol and saturated fat that comes with animal-based bacon. Tell us you don't want to dive into this savory sandwich right now—is it lunchtime yet?

Yield: 2 sandwiches

Prep time: 5 minutes | Total time: 5 minutes

4 slices sourdough or
white bread
2 dollops vegan mayo
1 batch Tofu Bacon (page
234)
1 tomato, sliced
2–4 large leaves romaine
lettuce
1 avocado, pitted and
sliced

1. Toast the bread and spread the vegan mayo on one side of each slice.
2. Assemble your sandwiches with the tofu bacon, tomato, lettuce, and avocado.

My Tips

Marinara Pizza

This classic pizza allows the flavors of Italy—garlic, basil, and tomato—to shine. We love topping our pie with a generous helping of shredded vegan mozzarella, briny olives, and a dash of red chili pepper flakes. You can use a store-bought crust (or dough) or make your own from scratch using the recipe on page 246.

Yield: 1 large pizza or 2 small pizzas (about 4 servings)
Prep time: 15 minutes | Cook time: 20 minutes | Total time: 35 minutes

1 cup pizza sauce

1 prepared pizza dough (store-bought or from the recipe on page 246), rolled to a large crust

1 tomato, very thinly sliced

Whole basil leaves, to taste

6 small cloves garlic, quartered

Vegan mozzarella cheese, sliced or shredded (optional)

¼ cup kalamata olives (optional)

1 tablespoon extra-virgin olive oil

Red chili pepper flakes, to taste

1. Preheat the oven to 375 degrees F.
2. Spread the pizza sauce evenly on the pizza dough or crust, leaving the outer rim exposed.
3. Add the tomato slices, basil leaves, garlic, vegan cheese (if using), and kalamata olives (if using).
4. Using a basting brush, brush the olive oil onto the outer rim of the crust.
5. Bake for 18 to 20 minutes (if you're using a prebaked store-bought crust, follow the baking directions on the package). If you are using cheese and it hasn't melted, broil for 1 to 2 minutes.
6. Remove from the oven, sprinkle with red chili pepper flakes, and enjoy immediately.

Friendly Suggestion: If you prefer your basil leaves raw on your pizza, add them after you have removed your pizza from the oven. They make a beautiful bright-green garnish.

My Tips

BBQ Pizza

 In our home, my husband and I often do a "make your own pizza" night. While my husband makes his ridiculously healthy with whole wheat dough, no vegan cheese, and mountains of veggies, I like this pizza much better. I make it with plant-based mozzarella cheese and vegan chicken nuggets, and if you're able to find these at your local grocery store, I recommend you use them, too.

Yield: 1 large pizza (4–6 servings)

Prep time: 15 minutes | Cook time: 25 minutes | Total time: 40 minutes

1 tablespoon canola oil

1 medium red onion, sliced

1 medium green bell pepper, sliced

4 large cloves garlic, thinly sliced

1 cup diced pineapple (we like canned)

1 cup barbecue sauce (store-bought or from the recipe on page 237)

1 prepared pizza dough (store-bought or from the recipe on page 246), rolled into a large crust

2 cups shredded vegan mozzarella cheese (optional)

8 frozen vegan chicken nuggets (any brand) (optional)

1. Preheat the oven to 375 degrees F.
2. In a large skillet over medium-high heat, heat the canola oil. Add the onion and bell pepper and sauté for about 5 minutes, until softened. Add the garlic and pineapple and sauté for 2 minutes.
3. Spread the barbecue sauce on the prepared pizza dough. Evenly sprinkle the bell pepper mixture and vegan cheese (if using) on the pizza. Evenly distribute the vegan chicken nuggets (if using) over the pizza.
4. Bake for 15 minutes (if you're using a prebaked store-bought crust, follow the baking directions on the package).

My Tips

Pesto Pizza

Pesto *anything* is amazing—right? This pizza uses our dee-lish walnut-based Pesto (page 227) to create a rich and flavorful five-star pizza experience. Topped with fresh tomatoes, garlic, and vegan mozzarella, it's simple to make and sure to impress. You can use a store-bought crust (or dough), or make your own from scratch using the recipe on page 246.

Yield: 1 large pizza or 2 small pizzas (about 4 servings)

Prep time: 15 minutes | Cook time: 30 minutes | Total time: 45 minutes

1 batch Pesto (page 227)

1 prepared pizza dough (store-bought or from the recipe on page 246), rolled into a large crust

1 to 2 cups shredded vegan mozzarella cheese (optional)

¾ cup halved cherry tomatoes

4 small cloves garlic, quartered

½ cup canned or marinated artichoke hearts, drained (optional)

Red chili pepper flakes, to taste

1. Preheat the oven to 375 degrees F.
2. Spread the pesto evenly on the pizza dough all the way to the edges.
3. Evenly sprinkle the pizza with the vegan cheese (if using), followed by the tomatoes, raw garlic, and artichoke hearts (if using).
4. Bake for 15 minutes (if you're using a prebaked store-bought crust, follow the baking directions on the package). Remove from the oven, sprinkle with red chili pepper flakes, and enjoy immediately.

My Tips

Warm & Cozy Soups

Soup is where we turn for comfort when we're sad, for celebration when we're happy, and for warmth when it's chilly outside—and hey, you might even find us at our local ramen house on a hot summer day. In short, soup is like a best friend that will always be there for you, and we love it. Especially when noodles are involved.

In this chapter we bring you along on a tour of our favorites. We've got classics like Split Pea Soup (page 107) and Chickenless Noodle Soup (page 108), and others that are more specialized, like our Lasagna Soup (page 111) and Spicy Udon Noodle Soup (page 116). And if there's one soup you absolutely must make, it's the Corn Chowder (page 104)—one of our recipe-testers' most beloved recipes.

Toni has been dubbed the "Soup Queen" because nearly every time we work together, she whips up the most delicious and flavorful soups using whatever happens to be in the fridge—no recipe required. We've even talked about writing an entire cookbook *all about soup*. But we'll start here.

Corn Chowder

We can't sing the praises of this soup enough. It's creamy-yet-chunky, and sings with the flavor of fresh summer corn. We've already had friends begging us for this recipe, and lucky for them—and you—it's really easy to make. If corn's not in season, don't worry—the frozen variety works just as well.

Yield: 4–6 servings

Prep time: 20 minutes | Cook time: 25 minutes | Total time: 45 minutes

You'll need: a blender and (optionally) an immersion blender

1½ tablespoons vegetable oil

1 small yellow onion, diced

2 large cloves garlic, minced

1 small red bell pepper, diced

½ medium jalapeño, seeded and minced

3 ribs celery, diced

1 pound red, russet, or Yukon Gold potatoes, chopped

4 cups corn kernels (frozen corn or fresh uncooked corn sliced directly off the cob— about 4 large ears), divided

4 cups rich vegetable broth (or equivalent amount of vegetable bouillon and water)

1½ teaspoons salt

2 cups unsweetened, plain plant-based milk

2 tablespoons chopped green onion, for garnish

Freshly ground black pepper, for garnish

1. In a large soup pot, heat the vegetable oil over medium-high heat.
2. Add the onion, garlic, bell pepper, jalapeño, and celery and sauté for 4 to 5 minutes, until the onion becomes translucent and tender.
3. Add the potatoes, 2 cups of the corn kernels, and vegetable broth. Bring to a boil and cook uncovered for about 20 minutes, until the potatoes are tender.
4. In a blender, combine the remaining 2 cups of corn kernels, salt, and plant-based milk and blend on high until smooth. Pour the mixture into the pot of soup, bring to a boil, and cook for an additional 5 minutes.
5. Remove the pot from the heat. Using an immersion blender, briefly blend some (but not all) of the soup. This will thicken the soup, but visible chunks of the ingredients should remain. (Alternatively, you can use a regular blender to purée half of the soup, and then add it back in.) Be careful not to overpurée, because you want plenty of chunkiness to remain in the soup.
6. Garnish each bowl with chopped green onion and freshly ground pepper.

Friendly Suggestion: If you have extra frozen corn kernels, toss them in the soup after blending.

My Tips

_____
_____
_____

Split Pea Soup

Packed with protein, fiber, and flavor, this wholesome soup is the ideal meal for chilly fall or winter nights. Fortunately, dried split peas are available all year round, so you can whip this up whenever you have a hankering for something warm and nourishing. And did you know that split peas are one of the most affordable foods on the planet?

Yield: 4–6 servings

Prep time: 20 minutes | Cook time: 1 hour | Total time: 1 hour and 20 minutes

You'll need: an immersion blender (optional)

1 tablespoon vegetable oil
1 large yellow onion, sliced
3 large carrots, diced
4 ribs celery, diced
1 large potato (any type), diced
2 bay leaves
1 teaspoon garlic powder
1 teaspoon ground black pepper
1 teaspoon dried thyme
7 cups vegetable broth (or equivalent amount of vegetable bouillon and water)
2 cups green split peas, rinsed and drained
Hot sauce, for serving (optional)

1. In a large soup pot, heat the vegetable oil over medium heat. Add the onion, carrots, and celery and sauté until the onion becomes translucent, about 5 minutes.

2. Add the potato, bay leaves, garlic powder, pepper, and thyme and stir well.

3. Add the vegetable broth and split peas. Bring to a boil, then reduce the heat to a high simmer, cover, and simmer vigorously for 40 minutes. Remove the lid and continue simmering for 20 more minutes or until the peas have softened and the soup has thickened.

4. Remove the bay leaves.

5. If you'd like a creamier soup, then, using an immersion blender, very briefly blend some (but not all) of the soup. This will thicken the soup, but visible chunks of the ingredients should remain. If you prefer a fully blended, creamy soup, you may continue blending until the desired consistency is achieved. Don't have an immersion blender? Don't worry! Once the soup cools, you can use a standard blender, or simply serve as is. Serve with hot sauce (if using).

My Tips

Chickenless Noodle Soup

There's nothing a steaming bowl of chickenless noodle soup can't cure, which is why we turn to this comforting dish whenever we're feeling under the weather. In place of chicken we use extra-firm tofu, which adds texture and substance.

Yield: 4 large servings

Prep time: 15 minutes | Cook time: 25 minutes | Total time: 40 minutes

1 tablespoon olive oil

1 medium yellow onion, diced

3 medium ribs celery, diced

3 medium carrots, sliced into thin rounds

4 medium cloves garlic, minced

½ teaspoon dried thyme

8 cups vegetable broth (or equivalent amount of vegetable bouillon and water)

1 bay leaf

8 ounces (half a 16-ounce package) of your favorite pasta

¾ teaspoon dried dill

8 ounces (half a 16-ounce block) extra-firm tofu, drained and sliced into small cubes

1 tablespoon chopped fresh parsley

1. In a large soup pot over medium-high heat, heat the olive oil. Add the onion, celery, carrots, garlic, and thyme and sauté until the onion becomes translucent, about 5 minutes.

2. Add the vegetable broth and the bay leaf and bring to a rolling boil. Allow to boil for at least 5 minutes.

3. Add the uncooked pasta to the pot and continue boiling until the pasta is cooked (using the cooking time suggested on your package of pasta).

4. As soon as the pasta is tender, remove the pot from heat, remove the bay leaf, and stir in the dill and tofu. Serve garnished with a sprinkle of fresh parsley.

Friendly Suggestion: If you like firmer tofu, which better replicates that chicken mouthfeel, you can bake the tofu with ½ teaspoon of salt and ½ teaspoon of ground black pepper at 425 degrees F for 10 to 15 minutes before adding it to the soup.

My Tips

Lasagna Soup

This soup is pure genius, using a much-beloved dish—lasagna—as a jumping-off point, and reimagining it as a meal you can eat with a spoon. Happily, it's *way* easier to make than lasagna, but just as hearty and flavorsome. It's also great for batch cooking as you can fill a pot and have leftovers for days. This recipe is in regular rotation in each of our kitchens, and we know you're going to love it, too!

Yield: 4 servings

Prep time: 20 minutes | Cook time: 30 minutes | Total time: 50 minutes

1 tablespoon extra-virgin olive oil

1 medium yellow onion, diced

3 medium cloves garlic, minced (or 1 teaspoon garlic powder)

1 red bell pepper, sliced into strips (or 1 cup frozen sliced bell peppers)

1 teaspoon dried basil

1 teaspoon dried oregano

4 cups low-sodium vegetable broth (or equivalent amount of vegetable bouillon and water)

2 cups marinara sauce (store-bought or from the recipe on page 228)

7 lasagna noodles (standard size)

8 ounces (half a 16-ounce block) extra-firm tofu, drained (or 1 cup sliced vegan Italian sausage or vegan beefy crumbles)

2 cups packed baby spinach

Salt and pepper, to taste

1. In a large soup pot over high heat, heat the olive oil. Add the onion and garlic and sauté for 2 minutes.

2. Lower the heat to medium, add the bell pepper, basil, and oregano, and sauté for another 10 minutes.

3. Add the vegetable broth and marinara sauce and bring the soup to a boil.

4. Once the soup is gently boiling, add the lasagna noodles. Roughly break the lasagna noodles into bite-sized chunks by hand into the pot. Crumble the tofu directly into the pot using your hands (or add the sliced vegan sausage or vegan beefy crumbles) and then reduce the heat to a high simmer. Simmer the soup until the pasta is cooked through, stirring frequently to prevent the lasagna noodles from sticking together. The time will vary depending on the type of lasagna pasta you chose, so cook according to the directions on the package and taste for doneness.

5. Once the pasta is cooked, add the spinach and stir to wilt.

6. Season with salt and pepper.

Minestrone

We've discovered the ultimate trifecta for a cozy night in: a snuggly sweater, a just-baked loaf of Sourdough Bread (page 249), and a steaming bowl of this loaded minestrone on the table. This tomatoey soup tastes even better the next day, when all the flavors have combined and settled, so it's perfect for plan-ahead meals.

Yield: 6–8 servings

Prep time: 15 minutes | Cook time: 40 minutes | Total time: 55 minutes

2 tablespoons vegetable oil

1 large yellow onion, diced

3 ribs celery, thinly sliced

2 carrots, thinly sliced

1 cup green beans (fresh or frozen), sliced into bite-sized chunks

4 large cloves garlic, minced

2 teaspoons dried oregano

1 large bay leaf

½ teaspoon ground cumin

6 cups vegetable broth (or equivalent amount of vegetable bouillon and water)

2 (14.5-ounce) cans diced tomatoes, with their juices

1 (15-ounce) can white beans, drained and rinsed

1 medium russet potato, diced (other potatoes will work too)

1 cup dry pasta in the shape of your choice (such as rotini or small shells)

Salt and pepper, to taste

1. In a large soup pot over medium-high heat, heat the vegetable oil. Add the onion, celery, carrots, and green beans. Sauté for 8 to 10 minutes, until the vegetables become tender.

2. Stir in the garlic, oregano, bay leaf, and cumin and cook for 2 minutes.

3. Pour in the vegetable broth (or bouillon and water), diced tomatoes with their juices, beans, and potatoes and bring to a boil. Lower the heat to medium and cook covered for about 15 minutes, until the potatoes are tender.

4. Stir in the pasta and cook uncovered for the amount of time suggested in the directions on the package.

5. Remove from the heat, remove the bay leaf, and sprinkle with salt and pepper.

My Tips

Our Favorite Chili

When I was younger, I would eat canned chili like it was going out of style. This updated rendition of the classic one-pot meal retains all the beefy chili goodness that I remember as a child, thanks to TVP (textured vegetable protein). It's chunky; packed with protein, veggies, and nutritious spices; and fabulous served alongside our Cornbread (page 253) or in our Cornbread Chili Casserole (page 82).

You can find TVP at many mainstream grocery stores, but vegan beefy crumbles will work, too (just skip step 1).

Yield: 8 servings

Prep time: 30 minutes | Cook time: 1 hour | Total time: 1 hour and 30 minutes

- ½ cup textured vegetable protein (TVP)
- 2 cups water, divided
- 2 tablespoons canola oil
- 1 small yellow onion, diced
- ½ medium green bell pepper, diced
- 4 medium cloves garlic, minced
- 1 tablespoon ground cumin
- 2 teaspoons chili powder
- ½ teaspoon dried oregano

- ¼ teaspoon cayenne pepper
- ¼ teaspoon ground black pepper
- 1 (14.5-ounce) can diced tomatoes, with their juices
- 2 (15-ounce) cans kidney beans, drained and rinsed
- 1 (15-ounce) can chickpeas, drained and rinsed
- ½ cup corn kernels (frozen corn or fresh

- uncooked corn sliced directly off the cob)
- 1 vegetable bouillon cube
- 1 (6-ounce) can tomato paste
- 2 tablespoons nutritional yeast
- 1 bay leaf
- Chopped cilantro, for garnish (optional)
- Finely diced red onion, for garnish (optional)

1. In a medium bowl, soak the textured vegetable protein in 1 cup of water for 30 minutes. Drain, press the water out, and set aside.

2. In a large nonstick pot over medium-high heat, heat the canola oil. Add the onion and bell pepper and sauté for about 5 minutes, until the onion becomes translucent. Add the TVP, garlic, cumin, chili powder, oregano, cayenne pepper, and black pepper and sauté for 3 minutes.

3. Stir in the tomatoes with their juices, kidney beans, chickpeas, corn kernels, 1 cup of water, bouillon cube, tomato paste, nutritional yeast, and bay leaf.

4. Bring the chili to a boil, cover, turn the heat to the lowest setting, and simmer for 1 hour, stirring occasionally to prevent burning. Remove the bay leaf before serving. Garnish with cilantro and diced red onion (if using).

Spicy Udon Noodle Soup

It's no secret that we are crazy for noodles! We love them when it's hot, and when it's cold, and especially when they're suspended in a piquant broth surrounded by perfectly cooked vegetables. You can find dried udon noodles in the Asian section of many grocery stores, or fresh udon noodles at many Asian markets. They vary considerably in size, shape, and consistency, so you might want to try a few different kinds to find your favorite.

Yield: 6 servings

Prep time: 15 minutes | Cook time: 20 minutes | Total time: 35 minutes

1 tablespoon canola oil

1 small yellow onion, diced

2 ribs celery, sliced

1 large carrot, julienned or diced

3 large cloves garlic, minced

1 cup bunashimeji or enoki mushrooms (long, skinny mushrooms) (optional)

9 cups water

3 vegetable bouillon cubes

2½ cups shredded napa or green cabbage

1 (12-ounce) package dry udon noodles

1 tablespoon Sriracha sauce

Ground black pepper, to taste

2 green onions, sliced, for garnish (optional)

½ sheet sushi nori (toasted seaweed), finely sliced, for garnish (optional)

1. In a large soup pot over medium-high heat, heat the canola oil. Add the onion, celery, carrot, garlic, and mushrooms (if using), and sauté, stirring occasionally, for 5 minutes or until the onion is tender and translucent.

2. Pour in the water and bring to a boil. Add the bouillon cubes, cabbage, and noodles, and cook for the amount of time suggested on the package.

3. Remove from the heat and stir in the Sriracha sauce and pepper.

4. Divide the soup among single-serving bowls. Garnish each bowl with a sprinkle of green onions and finely sliced sushi nori (if using them).

Friendly Suggestion: Make this soup stretch further by adding a drained and diced block of extra-firm tofu. It will give you a couple of extra servings to enjoy as leftovers, plus a boost of protein. Win-win.

> **My Tips**
>
> _____
>
> _____
>
> _____

Ramen

Japanese noodle soups hold a special place in our hearts. They've been the go-to meal in our friendship for rewarding ourselves after a hard day at work, for mending broken hearts, for celebrating, and for catching up on the details of our lives. It was really important to get this recipe right, and we *really, reeeally* got it right! We recommend using fresh ramen noodles because they are infinitely better than the dried packets and will give this soup a restaurant-quality feel. You can find fresh ramen in the refrigerated section at your local Asian market and at well-stocked grocery stores, though instant ramen noodles will do in a pinch.

May it be a comforting meal to you and yours for celebrating, sharing, and showing love.

Yield: 4 servings

Prep time: 20 minutes | Cook time: 45 minutes | Total time: 1 hour and 5 minutes

1 tablespoon canola oil
½ teaspoon toasted sesame oil
1 small yellow onion, diced
4 medium cloves garlic, minced
1 tablespoon minced ginger
1 tablespoon sesame seeds, ground with a mortar and pestle
7 cups water
3 vegetable bouillon cubes

2 teaspoons soy sauce
2 teaspoons miso
1 dried shiitake mushroom (fresh will work, too)
½ cup unsweetened, plain soy milk
1 (16-ounce package) fresh ramen noodles
½ cup corn kernels (frozen corn or fresh uncooked corn sliced directly off the cob), for garnish
½ cup bean sprouts, for garnish (optional)

4 heads baby bok choy, steamed, for garnish (optional)
1 sheet sushi nori (toasted seaweed), cut into short strips, for garnish
2 green onions, sliced, for garnish
Chili oil or red chili pepper flakes, to taste, for garnish (optional)

1. In a large soup pot over medium-high heat, heat the canola and sesame oils. Add the onion and sauté for 5 to 7 minutes, stirring occasionally, until the onion is translucent and tender. Add the garlic, ginger, and ground sesame seeds, lower the heat to medium, and sauté for 2 more minutes.

2. Add the water, bouillon cubes, soy sauce, miso, and mushroom. Increase the heat to high, bring the mixture to a boil, stir, and cover the pot. Reduce the heat to a simmer and simmer for 30 minutes.

3. Using a strainer, strain the broth into a large bowl. Make sure you press and squeeze all the juice out of the onions—that's the good stuff!

(Continues)

4. Discard the strained veggies and pour the broth back into the pot. Add the soy milk and bring to a rolling boil over high heat. Add the fresh ramen noodles and cook for 30 seconds. Serve the noodles and broth immediately in individual bowls, garnished with a spoonful of corn kernels, bean sprouts (if using), a baby bok choy head (if using), strips of nori, green onions, and chili oil or flakes (if using).

Love Your Leftovers: When using fresh ramen, only cook noodles for the number of portions you'll be serving, and if you plan to have leftovers, store the broth separately and cook the fresh noodles just before ladling the soup into bowls. They only take 30 seconds to cook in boiling broth, and it's a million times better this way!

My Tips

Apps, Snacks & Sides

Not sure what to make for that backyard barbecue, potluck, or family Thanksgiving? We've got you covered in this chapter.

A few of our favorites are Michael's Southern Collard Greens (page 154) (they're *packed* with flavor), pasta and potato salads (which earned stellar reviews from our testers), and our Rainbow Tofu Kebabs (page 134), which are a colorful addition to any barbecue.

We're also thrilled to include one of our favorite recipes of all time—Chloe's Spinach-Artichoke Dip (page 138), a guest recipe from chef Chloe Coscarelli that will blow your mind (and is surprisingly healthy).

Have fun complementing your dinner centerpiece with these lip-smacking sides, party-friendly appetizers, and tasty snacks.

Rainbow Spring Rolls with Peanut Dipping Sauce

We're going to let you in on a secret: those fancy spring rolls you've been ordering at Thai restaurants are unbelievably easy and affordable to make at home! Our recipe includes a rainbow of veggies to pack in tons of nutrition, but feel free to swap out ingredients for whatever you fancy. Not a fan of tofu? Leave it out and save yourself a step. Can't find vermicelli noodles? No worries, you can replace them with rice or leave them out completely and these will still taste incredible.

Yield: 5 rolls

Prep time: 45 minutes | Total time: 45 minutes

Peanut Dipping Sauce:

2 tablespoons soy sauce (not low-sodium)
2 tablespoons lime juice
1 tablespoon rice vinegar
2 teaspoons granulated sugar
½ teaspoon ground ginger
1 teaspoon garlic powder
¼ teaspoon red chili pepper flakes
½ cup creamy peanut butter
5 tablespoons water (use more or less to get the perfect desired consistency)

Spring Rolls:

2 ounces uncooked rice vermicelli noodles
4 ounces (one-quarter of a 16-ounce block) extra-firm tofu, drained (or baked tofu)
5 round rice papers (each about 8½ inches in diameter)
½ red bell pepper, thinly sliced
1 cup shredded carrots
½ yellow bell pepper, thinly sliced
⅓ cup fresh mint leaves
⅓ cup fresh cilantro leaves
½ cup shredded purple cabbage

1. To make the peanut dipping sauce, combine all the sauce ingredients except for the water in a medium bowl and whisk until well blended.
2. Add the water 1 tablespoon at a time until the perfect creamy, dippable peanut sauce consistency is achieved. Set the sauce aside while you make the rainbow spring rolls.
3. To make the spring rolls, cook the vermicelli noodles according to the directions on the package. Drain and rinse the noodles under cold water to prevent sticking, and place in a bowl of cold water until ready to use.

(Continues)

4. Clear a clean, flat work surface (such as a large cutting board or smooth countertop). Slice the tofu into strips (like skinny French fries).

5. Fill a large bowl or rimmed plate with warm water and bring it to your spring roll assembly area. Working one at a time, dip the rice paper into the warm water and submerge completely for about 4 seconds to soften. Don't leave it in the water too long or it will tear easily. Once removed from the water it will continue to soften over time. Transfer the rice paper to your work surface.

6. Assemble the fillings in the center of the rice paper, lined up in order by color. For instance: vermicelli noodles, tofu, red bell pepper slices, shredded carrots, yellow bell pepper slices, mint leaves, cilantro leaves, and shredded purple cabbage. Leave at least 1½ inches on all four sides bare for wrapping.

7. To wrap the spring roll, fold two opposite sides of the wrap over the fillings to create the closed ends of the roll. Then, starting from the vermicelli noodle end, use both hands to fold the rice paper over the noodles and begin to tightly roll the rice paper and fillings into a tube-shaped spring roll, being careful not to tear the rice paper. Repeat with the remaining rice paper wrappers and fillings.

8. Serve the spring rolls with the peanut dipping sauce. Enjoy immediately!

Friendly Suggestion: If serving at a party, slice the rolls in half as pictured to showcase the colorful interior. Just keep in mind that this will make them messier to eat unless they are very well wrapped.

Love Your Leftovers: These are best enjoyed fresh, but if you must save some for later, wrap individual rolls tightly in plastic wrap and store in the fridge.

My Tips

Jenn's Fried Tofu Wontons

This recipe comes from the kitchen of my friend Jenn Wong. We met at our local community college's veg club a decade ago, and I'm still using her recipes to this day. She's an excellent cook, and I'm glad to include something she's created.

    These wontons are best enjoyed immediately. Since this recipe makes a big batch, it's ideal to make during a party (invite your friends to help!) or for a large gathering.

Yield: 40 wontons

Prep time: 30 minutes | Cook time: 45 minutes | Total time: 1 hour and 15 minutes

You'll need: a food processor

½ medium yellow onion
1 small carrot
¼ cup teriyaki sauce
1½ tablespoons soy sauce
8 ounces (half a 16-ounce block) extra-firm tofu, drained
½–1 cup vegetable oil, for frying and deep-frying
1 (50-count) package wonton wraps (you'll use 40)
Your favorite sauce for dipping (we like sweet and sour)

1. In a food processor, pulse the onion and carrot until minced.
2. In a large bowl, combine the teriyaki sauce and soy sauce and add the tofu. (Or, if you bought tofu packaged in a plastic tub, you can return the tofu to its package after draining and pour the sauces right on top. Set the container on a plate.) Marinate the tofu for 10 minutes.
3. Coat the bottom of a large skillet with 1 tablespoon of vegetable oil and heat over medium-high heat. Add the minced carrot and onion to the pan. Using your fingers, crumble the tofu into the pan and then pour in any remaining marinade.
4. Constantly flip the crumbled tofu mixture until it is thoroughly cooked for about 4 or 5 minutes. Allow the mixture to cool.
5. When you're ready to assemble the wontons, have a small dish of cold water ready near your work area. Place 1 tablespoon of the cooled tofu mixture in the center of a wonton wrap. Fold the wrapper in half over the filling to form a triangle and use a small amount of water around the

edges to seal the tofu mixture in. You can leave the wonton as a triangle or you may fold the two matching acute corners of the triangle over one another on top of the stuffed center, as pictured. Repeat until all the filling is gone.

6. In a large pan, add enough oil to cover the wontons and heat over medium-high heat. Working in batches, fry the wontons until both sides are lightly browned for about 1 minute, remove the finished wontons, and allow them to cool. Repeat until all the wontons are fried.

7. Serve with your favorite dipping sauce.

Tester Tip: "I popped our leftover wontons in the freezer. The following day I reheated them in the oven and *oh my*! They were wonderful once again!" —Karen B.

My Tips

Mashed Potatoes

These are the *best* mashed potatoes. Loaded with garlic and mashed to creamy perfection, these pair wonderfully with our flavorful Mushroom Gravy (page 231). They also serve as the delectable topping to our Shepherd's Pie (page 69). Your biggest challenge with this recipe will be not eating the whole pot. You've been warned!

Yield: 6–8 servings

Prep time: 10 minutes | Cook time: 25 minutes | Total time: 35 minutes

4 pounds russet potatoes (4–5 large potatoes), cut into 1-inch pieces
8 medium cloves garlic, peeled
1 cup unsweetened, plain plant-based milk
¼ cup vegan butter
1 teaspoon salt
½ teaspoon ground black pepper

1. Place the potatoes and whole garlic cloves in a large pot and completely submerge them in cold water. Bring to a boil over medium-high heat and then boil for 20 to 25 minutes, until the potatoes are completely tender.

2. Drain the potatoes and garlic in a colander and return them to the pot. Add the plant-based milk, vegan butter, salt, and pepper.

3. Mash the potatoes and garlic with a potato masher or a large and sturdy fork until they reach your desired consistency.

Friendly Suggestion: You can peel some or all of the potatoes if you'd like, but we like our mashed potatoes best with the skins left on.

My Tips

Fried Rice

The next time you're craving Chinese take-out, skip the delivery and make this fried rice at home instead! We use hand-crumbled tofu, which takes on egglike characteristics, and toasted sesame oil to give it that classic umami flavor. Just watch out—it's addictive!

Yield: 2–3 servings

Prep time: 20 minutes | Cook time: 15 minutes | Total time: 35 minutes

1 tablespoon toasted sesame oil

½ medium yellow onion, diced

2 large cloves garlic, minced

½ cup frozen peas

½ cup finely diced carrots

8 ounces (half a 16-ounce block) extra-firm tofu, pressed and broken up into crumbles

2½ cups cooked medium- or long-grain white rice

3 tablespoons soy sauce

Optional Toppings:

Sriracha sauce
Sliced green onions

1. In a large nonstick pan over medium-high heat, heat the sesame oil. Add the onion, garlic, peas, carrots, and crumbled tofu, and sauté until the onion becomes tender and translucent, about 5 minutes.

2. Add the cooked rice and soy sauce. Sauté for 5 to 8 minutes, stirring frequently, until the rice appears golden and gently fried.

3. Top with any optional toppings.

My Tips

Rainbow Tofu Kebabs

Kebabs aren't just for outdoor summer barbecues; they're an anytime meal-on-a-stick you can make in the oven, rain or shine! We like to serve these atop a bed of fluffy rice, but you might slide the tofu and veggies off the skewer and serve them on a salad or stuffed in a pita.

Yield: 8 kebabs

Prep time: 30 minutes | Cook time: 25 minutes | Total time: 12+ hours

You'll need: kebab skewers (metal if grilling outdoors)

Advance prep required (marinate the tofu)

1 (16-ounce) block extra-firm tofu, pressed
1 batch marinade of choice (such as Orange Ginger Marinade, page 241; Teriyaki Sauce, page 240; or Barbecue Sauce, page 237)

8 cherry tomatoes
1 orange bell pepper, sliced into 8 chunks
1 yellow bell pepper, sliced into 8 chunks
1 medium zucchini, sliced into 8 rounds
½ large red onion, cut into 8–16 wedges

1. Cut the tofu into 16 cubes. Pierce the tofu cubes on all sides with a toothpick; this will allow the marinade to reach farther into the tofu, imparting more flavor. Place the tofu in a large bowl or a plastic bag, cover with your chosen marinade, and allow the tofu to marinate in the refrigerator for at least 12 hours. The longer it marinates, the more flavorful it will be.
2. Preheat the oven to 400 degrees F. Line a baking sheet with parchment paper or a silicone mat.
3. One by one, skewer the ingredients in the following order: cherry tomato, marinated tofu, orange bell pepper, yellow bell pepper, marinated tofu, zucchini, and one or two onion slices. Place each assembled kebab on the prepared baking sheet.
4. Spoon additional marinade over the tofu and unmarinated veggies.
5. Bake for 25 minutes or until the vegetables are cooked through to your liking.

Outdoor grill instructions:

1. When grilling the kebabs, make sure to use metal skewers.
2. Place the skewers on a heated grill and grill for about 10 minutes, flipping as needed, until you see grill marks on the tofu and the veggies are cooked to your liking.

My Tips

Nacho Cheese Sauce

This nacho cheese is the perfect chip dip for game-day parties. The texture is a crazy-close match to ballpark nacho cheese, except it's made entirely from plants (primarily potatoes and carrots). Serve it alongside tortilla chips for dunking, or drizzle it atop a plate of chips piled high with toppings for classic nachos, and get ready for a home run. We love to add some chunky salsa for extra pizzazz.

Yield: 3 cups

Prep time: 20 minutes | Cook time: 30 minutes | Total time: 50 minutes

You'll need: a high-powered blender

2 cups peeled and diced potatoes (any type)
½ cup chopped carrots
3 tablespoons extra-virgin olive oil
½ large yellow onion, roughly chopped
½ jalapeño, seeded (add more or less to adjust spiciness)
4 medium cloves garlic, roughly chopped
½ cup nutritional yeast
¼ teaspoon ground turmeric
1 tablespoon lemon juice
1 teaspoon salt
Tortilla chips, for serving

1. In a medium pot, cover the potatoes and carrots with water. Place the pot over medium-high heat, bring to a boil, and boil for about 20 minutes, until the veggies are soft. Before draining, add ½ cup of the hot water from the pot to a high-powered blender. Drain the remaining water and add the potatoes and carrots to the blender.

2. Heat the olive oil in a small pan over medium heat. Add the onion and jalapeño and sauté for 2 minutes. Add the garlic and continue sautéing for 3 more minutes, stirring frequently. Remove the pan from the heat, allow the onion mixture to cool for a few minutes, and add it to the blender.

3. Add the nutritional yeast, turmeric, lemon juice, and salt to the blender and blend until you have a completely smooth nacho cheese sauce. Serve fresh with tortilla chips.

Friendly Suggestion: For a nacho cheese sauce with kick, mix in ¼ cup of chunky salsa (of your desired spiciness level) after blending.

My Tips

Chloe's Spinach-Artichoke Dip

Chloe Coscarelli has been an inspiration to both of us for many years, and her first cookbook, *Chloe's Kitchen*, is one of our favorites. We come back to her Spinach-Artichoke Dip whenever we're craving something decadent and savory to eat with chips, bread, or crackers. This magical recipe has all the decadence of classic spinach-artichoke dip, only it's made using *far* healthier ingredients. A staple at our parties, potlucks, picnics, and game day, it always gets rave reviews!

Yield: 8–10 servings

Prep time: 20 minutes | Cook time: 40 minutes | Total time: 1 hour

You'll need: a food processor

2 tablespoons olive oil
1 medium yellow onion, roughly chopped
3 medium cloves garlic, minced
½ teaspoon red chili pepper flakes (optional)
1 (5-ounce) package baby spinach
1 (14-ounce) block silken (also called "soft") tofu, drained
½ cup nutritional yeast
2 tablespoons lemon juice
1 teaspoon dried basil
1½ teaspoons salt
½ teaspoon ground black pepper
12 ounces canned, marinated, or frozen artichoke hearts, drained
Bread or tortilla chips, for serving

1. Preheat the oven to 350 degrees F. Lightly grease a 1-quart baking dish.
2. In a large skillet, heat the olive oil over medium-high heat and sauté the onion until soft, about 5 minutes. Add the garlic and red chili pepper flakes and cook for 2 more minutes. Reduce the heat to medium-low, add the spinach, and cook, stirring gently, just until the spinach is wilted, about 3 minutes.
3. In a food processor, blend the tofu, nutritional yeast, lemon juice, basil, salt, and pepper until smooth. Add the artichokes and the spinach mixture, and pulse about 15 times. Transfer to the prepared baking dish.
4. Bake for 30 minutes or until lightly browned on top. Let cool a few minutes, then serve with bread or tortilla chips.

My Tips

Stephanie's Deviled Potatoes

Farewell deviled eggs, hello deviled potatoes! Whether you're looking for an Easter brunch appetizer or just a comforting dish to wow your friends and family, this recipe has your back. It makes a big batch of thirty deviled potatoes that are a perfect finger food to serve at any party. This recipe was inspired by our dear friend and fellow vegan food blogger Stephanie Dreyer and is widely loved by vegans and omnivores alike.

Yield: 30 deviled potatoes

Prep time: 30 minutes | Cook time: 1 hour | Total time: 1 hour and 30 minutes

You'll need: a food processor, a small melon baller, and a piping bag and tip

15 egg-sized yellow potatoes (such as Yukon Gold)
1 tablespoon olive oil
½ teaspoon salt
¾ cup cooked cannellini beans, drained and rinsed
2 tablespoons lemon juice
1 tablespoon Dijon mustard
1 teaspoon ground turmeric
¼ cup plus 1 tablespoon vegan mayo
¼ teaspoon salt (use black salt if you have it)
¼ teaspoon ground black pepper
¼ cup chopped chives, for garnish
Paprika, for sprinkling

1. Preheat the oven to 350 degrees F. Line a baking sheet with parchment paper or a silicone mat.
2. Halve the potatoes. In a large bowl, toss the potatoes with the olive oil and salt until evenly coated. Spread the potatoes cut side up on the prepared baking sheet. Roast in the oven for 1 hour or until soft.
3. Cool the potatoes for 5 minutes. Using a melon baller, scoop out a small half sphere from each potato half, being careful not to scoop through to the skin. Set aside the potato halves.
4. In a food processor, blend the removed potato, cannellini beans, lemon juice, mustard, turmeric, vegan mayo, ¼ teaspoon of salt (black salt if you have it), and pepper until completely smooth and creamy.
5. Using a piping bag with a tip, pipe the creamy yellow mixture into the hole in each potato half to fill, swirling to create a decorative raised peak.
6. Garnish with the chives and sprinkle with paprika.

Tester Tip: "I love to use Indian black salt (kala namak) in this recipe to bring out that "eggy" flavor. —Amanda M.

Quinoa Tots

When you think of quinoa, you probably don't envision crispy, golden-brown nuggets that resemble the tots you used to eat as a kid. We were skeptical at first, too, but that all changed with the first bite. These are chewy, generously seasoned, and hold together beautifully. Quinoa is a complete protein, meaning that it contains all the essential amino acids, making these a nutritious, protein-rich snack, too. These tots pair perfectly with our Thousand Island Dressing (page 239) or your favorite dip.

Yield: 16 quinoa tots

Prep time: 10 minutes | Cook time: 10 minutes | Total time: 30 minutes

2 cups cooked quinoa, cooled (see box on page 144)
½ cup finely diced yellow onion
¼ cup finely chopped chives
½ cup all-purpose flour
1 teaspoon salt
½ teaspoon red chili pepper flakes
3 tablespoons unsweetened, plain plant-based milk
1 tablespoon lemon juice
Canola oil (for panfrying)
Vegetable oil spray (for air-fryer option)
Panko bread crumbs (for air-fryer option)

1. In a large bowl, thoroughly combine the quinoa, onion, chives, flour, salt, and red chili pepper flakes. Mix in the plant-based milk and lemon juice.

2. Using your hands, roll the quinoa mixture into 1-inch balls, squeezing tightly in your hands as you go to get the air bubbles out and form a dough. Place the formed balls on a tray or plate. Put them in the freezer for 5 minutes. (If you don't have room in your freezer, you can chill them in your refrigerator for 15 minutes.)

3. Coat a large pan with canola oil and place over medium-high heat. Add the tots in batches and lightly press on each of them with a spatula to flatten them a little. If necessary, oil the spatula to prevent sticking. Cook the tots for 5 minutes until the bottom is golden brown and appears gently fried, and then flip them over. Lower the heat to medium and cook for 5 more minutes. (Alternatively, you can bake these tots on a greased nonstick pan at 400 degrees F for 30 minutes, flipping them halfway. Be sure to flatten them before baking.)

(Continues)

Don't know how to make quinoa? Here's an easy recipe:

1. Rinse ⅔ cup of dry quinoa in cold water using a fine-mesh strainer. Add the quinoa and 1⅓ cups of water to a medium pot with a lid. Bring to a boil, uncovered, over high heat. Cover with the lid and reduce the heat to low. Cook for 20 minutes.
2. Allow to cool before using for this recipe.

Tester Tip: "I cooked half of the batch in the air fryer with incredible results. Nice and crispy all the way around the tots. For a dipping sauce (they are plenty flavorful as is, but the sauce provides a nice cooling sensation), I mixed a bit of Sriracha sauce into some vegan mayo." —Justin A.

Air-fryer option:

1. Proceed with the recipe through the end of step 2, but do not cook the tots. Preheat the air fryer to 400 degrees F (about 5 minutes).
2. While the fryer is heating, coat the balls in panko bread crumbs.
3. Lightly spray the tots and the fryer basket with vegetable oil and cook for 10 minutes.

My Tips

Pesto Crostini

If you've been searching for the perfect appetizer to serve at your next gathering, we've got it. This classic pesto crostini topped with juicy cherry tomatoes is as delightful to look at as it is to devour. We dare you and your guests to eat just one!

Yield: 15–20 crostini

Prep time: 15 minutes | Cook time: 10 minutes | Total time: 25 minutes

1 sourdough baguette
½ batch Pesto (page 227)
15–20 fresh basil leaves
20 cherry tomatoes, sliced in half
Pinch of red chili pepper flakes, to taste
15 kalamata olives, sliced (optional)

1. Preheat the oven to 375 degrees F.
2. Using a serrated knife, cut the baguette into diagonal slices that are about ⅓ inch thick. Place the slices on a baking sheet, spread each with the pesto, and bake for 10 minutes or until toasted and golden brown.
3. Remove from the oven and top each crostini slice with a fresh basil leaf, sliced tomatoes, red chili pepper flakes, and sliced kalamata olives (if using). Assemble on a serving platter and enjoy fresh.

Friendly Suggestion: These are best enjoyed fresh since they lose their appealing texture in the fridge once assembled.

My Tips

Classic Pasta Salad

This picnic-ready macaroni salad will bring familiarity and classic flavor to any gathering. Plus, it's made with an egg-free, plant-based mayo, so it's cholesterol-free. We like this pared-down recipe, but there's plenty of room for making it your own with extras like olives or pickles. The longer it sits in the refrigerator, the tastier this dish becomes. We recommend overnight, if you can hold out that long.

Yield: 8 servings

Prep time: 15 minutes | Cook time: 15 minutes | Total time: 1 hour and 30 minutes

1 (16-ounce) package of your favorite pasta (we love macaroni or ditalini)
¾ cup vegan mayo
1 teaspoon apple cider vinegar
2 tablespoons yellow mustard
1¼ teaspoons salt
½ teaspoon ground black pepper
2 celery ribs, thinly sliced
1 small red onion, finely diced
1 red bell pepper, diced

1. In a large pot of boiling water, cook the pasta according to the directions on the package. Drain the pasta, rinse with cold water, and allow to cool.
2. In a large bowl, combine the vegan mayo, apple cider vinegar, mustard, salt, pepper, celery, red onion, and bell pepper, and thoroughly mix together.
3. Add the cooled pasta and mix until well combined.
4. Place the macaroni salad in the refrigerator overnight or for at least 1 hour.

 "I love adding kalamata olives and ¼ cup of chopped fresh parsley for an additional flavor dimension and a pop of green."

Tester Tip: "I added 2 cans of chickpeas for protein to make this a nutritionally complete meal that can be eaten alone!" —Taylor W.

My Tips

Green Bean Casserole

I know, green beans aren't for everyone. Toni is in that camp, but I personally *love* them—especially in green bean casseroles at Thanksgiving. But in my eyes, the ultimate green bean casserole strikes a balance between too-soft and too-crisp green beans, creating a nice amount of creamy filling.

Yield: 8 servings

Prep time: 25 minutes | Cook time: 20 minutes | Total time: 45 minutes

You'll need: a high-powered blender

2 pounds fresh green beans

3 cups vegetable broth (or equivalent amount of vegetable bouillon and water), divided

½ cup raw cashews

¼ teaspoon salt

½ teaspoon ground black pepper

½ cup vegan butter

1 small onion, diced

2 cups button mushrooms, sliced or diced

4 medium cloves garlic, roughly chopped

½ cup all-purpose flour

2 cups crispy fried onions (we use store-bought)

1. To prepare the green beans, wash them, trim the stem ends, cut them in half, place them in a steamer basket, and steam for 7 minutes. Remove the green beans from the steamer, rinse them with ice-cold water to preserve the green color, and set aside.

2. In a high-powered blender, combine 1 cup of the vegetable broth and the cashews and blend on high until smooth. Blend in the remaining 2 cups of vegetable broth, salt, and pepper and set aside.

3. Preheat the oven to 375 degrees F.

4. In a large pot over medium-high heat, melt the vegan butter. Add the onion, mushrooms, and garlic and sauté for 5 minutes, stirring occasionally. Add the flour and whisk to create a roux. Continue to whisk the thickened roux constantly for 3 minutes. Add the broth and cashew mixture and whisk continuously for 2 to 3 minutes, until thickened (thickening will happen fast and suddenly, so be sure to turn off the heat just as the mixture gets thick enough).

5. Spoon the green beans and the creamy mixture into a 9 × 13-inch baking dish and mix until well combined. Top with an even layer of fried onions and bake for 20 minutes.

Stuffing

No holiday dinner is complete without stuffing, so we set about perfecting a recipe that we and our loved ones could enjoy year after year. This is it! When baked, it gets a decadent bread pudding texture at the bottom and becomes nice and crispy on top. We love it with our Mashed Potatoes (page 130) and Mushroom Gravy (page 231). We hope this becomes a staple on your holiday dinner table, just as it has at ours.

Yield: 8 servings

Prep time: 20 minutes | Cook time: 1 hour and 5 minutes | Total time: 1 hour and 25 minutes

Advance prep required (allow the bread crumbs to dry)

- 1 (16-ounce) loaf French bread
- 2 cups vegetable broth (or equivalent amount of vegetable bouillon and water)
- 1 tablespoon ground flaxseed meal
- ½ cup vegan butter, plus additional for greasing the dish
- 3 medium ribs celery, diced
- 1 medium yellow onion, diced
- 1 medium Granny Smith apple, cored and finely diced
- ⅓ cup finely chopped fresh parsley
- 2 teaspoons poultry seasoning

1. Cut the bread loaf into small (bite-sized) cubes, spread the bread cubes across a large baking sheet, and leave them out overnight or for at least 12 hours. The next day, preheat the oven to 250 degrees F and bake for 30 minutes to fully dry out the bread. Grease a 9 × 13-inch baking dish with vegan butter. Transfer the dried bread cubes to the prepared baking dish and set aside.

2. In a medium bowl, whisk together the broth and flaxseed meal. Set aside for at least 10 minutes.

3. Preheat the oven to 375 degrees F.

4. In a medium pan over medium-high heat, melt the vegan butter. Add the celery, onion, and apple and sauté, mixing occasionally, for 5 minutes or until tender.

5. Pour the sautéed veggie mixture and the vegetable broth mixture evenly over the bread in the baking dish, and sprinkle evenly with the parsley and poultry seasoning. Using your hands, mix to evenly coat.

6. Cover with aluminum foil and bake for 40 minutes. Remove the foil and bake for another 40 minutes. Allow to cool for 15 minutes before serving.

My Tips

Michael's Southern Collard Greens

These smoky southern collards are a delicious way to get your greens in and will make your entire house smell incredible. This recipe comes from the kitchen of our friend Michael Wallace, who is an amazing home cook as well as one of our superstar cookbook recipe testers. We love turning up the heat on our dishes, so these collard greens pack a spicy kick. If you're not a fan of spice, you can simply cut back on the red chili pepper flakes and still enjoy the southern-comfort flavors of this dish.

Yield: 2–3 servings

Prep time: 15 minutes | Cook time: 40 minutes | Total time: 55 minutes

2 tablespoons olive oil (or vegetable oil)

1 medium yellow onion, diced

3 large cloves garlic, minced

2 very ripe medium heirloom tomatoes, diced

1 large bunch collard greens, destemmed and cut into 1-inch-wide strips

¼ cup vegetable broth (or equivalent amount of vegetable bouillon and water)

1 teaspoon smoked paprika

1 teaspoon red chili pepper flakes (reduce if you don't really love spice)

¼ teaspoon salt (plus additional to taste, if desired)

¼ teaspoon ground black pepper

1. Coat the bottom of a medium pan or pot (with a lid) with olive oil and place over medium heat.
2. Add the onion and sauté until it is tender and translucent, about 5 minutes. Stir frequently to prevent burning. (You can add a pinch of salt to draw out the liquid, which also helps the onion soften.)
3. Add the garlic and stir for about 1 minute more, until fragrant.
4. Stir in the tomatoes and cook until they are soft, about 3 minutes.
5. Add the collard greens and vegetable broth and stir well. Reduce the heat to low and cover the pot. Cook for about 15 minutes, until the greens are wilted. Stir in the paprika, red chili pepper flakes, salt, and pepper. Cover the pot again and cook for another 15 minutes.

Friendly Suggestion: If you want less "gravy," uncover the pot with about 5 minutes left.

Classic Caesar Salad

This flavorful Caesar salad will have even the staunchest salad haters begging for seconds. Made with our tangy Caesar Dressing (page 243), it offers irresistibly satisfying crunch and texture with every healthy bite.

Yield: 4–6 servings

Prep time: 5 minutes | Total time: 5 minutes

3 hearts romaine lettuce, roughly chopped
⅓ cup Caesar Dressing (page 243)
¾ cup vegan croutons
2 tablespoons roasted sunflower seeds (no shells)
Freshly ground black pepper

In a large bowl, mix together the chopped lettuce and Caesar dressing. Top with croutons, sunflower seeds, and freshly ground black pepper.

Why It Works: We use roasted sunflower seeds in place of flaked vegan Parmesan cheese because they lend richness and a flavorful bite to the salad.

My Tips

Potato Salad

This traditional potato salad is incredibly easy to make with just six ingredients (plus salt and pepper). We've served it at parties, barbecues, potlucks, and weeknight dinners and it's always a big hit.

Yield: 8–10 servings

Prep time: 20 minutes | Cook time: 20 minutes | Total time: 1 hour and 40 minutes

3 or 4 large russet potatoes (about 1½ pounds), cut into 1-inch cubes

¾ cup vegan mayo

1½ tablespoons yellow mustard

2 large ribs celery, thinly sliced

1 small red onion, finely diced

1 large, crispy dill pickle, diced

Salt and pepper, to taste

1. In a large pot of boiling water over high heat, cook the potatoes for about 20 minutes, until they're soft and tender.

2. Drain the potatoes and spread them out on a plate or baking sheet to cool for 10 minutes.

3. In a large bowl, combine the potatoes, vegan mayo, mustard, celery, onion, pickle, salt, and pepper and thoroughly mix together.

4. Place the potato salad in the refrigerator overnight or for at least 1 hour.

Love Your Leftovers: The longer this sits in the refrigerator, the tastier it gets. It might test your patience, but we recommend overnight!

Friendly Suggestion: For an extra-creamy potato salad, stir in an additional 1 to 2 tablespoons of vegan mayo.

My Tips

_____

_____

_____

Mexican Rice

I've been making this recipe forever! It's a family favorite, and it's also one of my most popular recipes on PlantBasedonaBudget.com. It's deceptively simple, yet immensely flavorful. Try serving it as a side with our Beefy Tacos (page 84), in burritos, or topped with a big pile of steamed or stir-fried veggies and hot sauce.

Yield: 4 servings

Prep time: 10 minutes | Cook time: 35 minutes | Total time: 45 minutes

1 teaspoon vegetable oil
½ medium yellow onion, diced
2 small cloves garlic, minced
1 cup uncooked medium-grain white rice
½ cup tomato sauce
1 teaspoon salt
1½ cups water
Sprinkle of ground black pepper

1. In a medium pan with a lid, heat the vegetable oil over medium-high heat. Add the onion and garlic and sauté for 5 minutes or until the onion becomes tender and translucent.

2. Add the uncooked rice and sauté, stirring occasionally, for 2 to 3 minutes, until the rice is golden.

3. Add the tomato sauce, salt, water, and pepper, and stir.

4. Bring the mixture to a boil, cover the pan with the lid, and reduce the heat to low. Simmer for 20 minutes. Once you cover the rice, do not remove the lid.

5. Remove from the heat and fluff the rice.

Friendly Suggestion: When preparing the rice, it's important to keep the lid on the pan, since the steam is what does the cooking.

My Tips

Coleslaw

This colorful coleslaw is a perennial crowd-pleaser at barbecues. It tastes great on its own, but it's also delish served on our Black Bean Burgers (page 87) or Jackfruit "Pulled Pork" Sandwich (page 88). To shred the carrots and cabbage quickly and easily, we recommend using the shredding disk attachment on your food processor. To shred the carrots, use the shredding blade, and to shred the cabbage, slice into small wedges and use the slicing blade (which is usually on the opposite side). Of course, you may also buy pre-shredded veggies or use a cheese grater.

Yield: 4–6 servings

Prep time: 20 minutes | Total time: 20 minutes

1 large carrot, shredded
½ small head green cabbage, shredded
¼ small head purple cabbage, shredded
½ cup plus 1 tablespoon vegan mayo
1½ tablespoons lemon juice
½ tablespoon apple cider vinegar
1½ tablespoons granulated sugar
¼ teaspoon salt
Ground black pepper, to taste

1. In a large bowl, combine the shredded carrot and cabbage.
2. In a small bowl, whisk together the vegan mayo, lemon juice, apple cider vinegar, sugar, salt, and pepper until they are thoroughly mixed and no clumps remain.
3. Add the mayo mixture to the cabbage mixture and toss to evenly coat.

> **My Tips**
> _____
> _____
> _____

Meal Prepping Tip: This makes a large batch of coleslaw that can be stored in the fridge and added to meals all week long. Enjoy as a side or in sandwiches.

Desserts

Decadent chocolate mousse. Fudgy brownies. Ultra-rich milkshakes. We dive deep into the land of sweets in this chapter and can't wait to bring you with us.

In the pages to come, you'll discover the magic of Michelle's grandmother's famous cookies, made vegan (Grandma's Cookies, page 179); Toni's famous super-creamy Pumpkin Chocolate Pie (page 176); our go-to healthy sweet treat (Chocolate Peanut Butter Milkshake, page 196), and more.

Of course, we're also covering the basics, including how to make a basic vegan cake, vegan cupcakes, and vegan frosting.

So what are you waiting for? Tie up that apron and let's get baking!

Chocolate Cupcakes

Everyone who tastes these fluffy chocolate cupcakes falls in love at first bite. For a double-chocolate wallop that will impress your dining companions, top them with our Chocolate Frosting (page 169), which pipes beautifully. Have fun decorating these to fit any occasion by adding fancy vegan sprinkles, popping a cherry or strawberry on top, or even piping a filling into the center of the cupcakes once they're out of the oven (peanut butter and strawberry jam fillings are especially scrumptious).

Yield: 15 cupcakes

Prep time: 15 minutes | Cook time: 23 minutes | Total time: 38 minutes

1 cup unsweetened, plain soy milk
1 tablespoon ground flaxseed meal
½ tablespoon apple cider vinegar
1½ cups all-purpose flour
1 cup granulated sugar
⅓ cup cocoa powder
1 teaspoon baking soda
½ teaspoon baking powder
½ teaspoon salt
⅓ cup canola oil
2 teaspoons vanilla extract
½ cup water
1 batch Chocolate Frosting (page 169) or Buttercream Frosting (page 175)
Vegan sprinkles (optional)

1. Preheat the oven to 350 degrees F. Line muffin pans with paper or silicone liners.
2. In a medium bowl, whisk together the soy milk, flaxseed meal, and apple cider vinegar. Set aside for 10 minutes to curdle and thicken.
3. In a large bowl, combine the flour, sugar, cocoa powder, baking soda, baking powder, and salt.
4. After the soy milk mixture has sat for 10 minutes, add the canola oil, vanilla extract, and water to the soy milk mixture and whisk together. Pour the wet mixture into the large bowl of dry ingredients and mix just until a batter forms, being careful not to overmix.
5. Pour the batter into the cupcake liners, filling each three-quarters full. Bake for 23 minutes or until a toothpick inserted in the center comes out clean.
6. Allow the cupcakes to cool in the pans for a few minutes and then transfer them from the pan to a cooling rack. Let the cupcakes come to room temperature before frosting. Spread with your choice of frosting and top with sprinkles (if using).

Friendly Suggestion: If you want to decorate your cupcakes with fancy piping, we recommend making a double batch of the Chocolate Frosting recipe. Chill the frosted cupcakes once they're decorated so the frosting hardens and holds its shape.

My Tips

_____

_____

_____

Chocolate Frosting

This thick buttercream frosting spreads and pipes wonderfully on cooled cakes and cupcakes. Try it with our Birthday Cake (page 170) and Chocolate Cupcakes (page 166). If you'd like a thinner frosting, simply add additional soy milk (½ teaspoon at a time). For a thicker frosting, add additional powdered sugar. You can also pop this frosting in the fridge and it will firm up to a thicker consistency that's ideal for piping.

Yield: frosting for 12 cupcakes (about 2½ cups)

Prep time: 10 minutes | Total time: 10 minutes

You'll need: an electric hand mixer

⅓ cup cocoa powder
2 cups powdered sugar
¼ cup vegan butter, chilled
¼ cup vegetable shortening (such as Crisco)
2 teaspoons vanilla extract
2½ tablespoons unsweetened, plain soy milk, divided

In a large bowl, sift together the cocoa powder and powdered sugar. Add the butter, shortening, vanilla extract, and 1½ tablespoons of the soy milk. Whip together using an electric hand mixer. Slowly whip in the remaining 1 tablespoon of soy milk as needed, ½ tablespoon at a time, until the mixture has the consistency of thick frosting. Continue whipping until the frosting is fluffy and no lumps remain.

Friendly Suggestion: You're welcome to use ½ cup of vegan butter, rather than ¼ cup of butter and ¼ cup of shortening.

My Tips

Birthday Cake

We've been on a quest for the ultimate vegan cake recipe for years, and finally found it in this recipe developed by vegan baking aficionado Kathy Chrzaszcz for WorldofVegan.com. We use any special occasion as an excuse to make it, and love to have fun with the recipe by adding vegan sprinkles to the batter to create a "confetti cake" effect, or by decorating the top with fresh flowers, fruit, or chocolate drizzles.

Yield: 8–10 servings

Prep time: 30 minutes | Cook time: 30 minutes | Total time: 1 hour

You'll need: three 8-inch cake pans and an electric stand mixer or hand mixer

2 cups soy milk (any variety), at room temperature

1 tablespoon apple cider vinegar

2 cups all-purpose flour

1 tablespoon baking powder

1 teaspoon baking soda

½ teaspoon salt

1⅓ cups granulated sugar

¾ cup vegan butter, at room temperature

1 tablespoon vanilla extract

1 batch Buttercream Frosting (page 175) or 2 batches Chocolate Frosting (page 169)

Optional Decorating Ideas:

Fresh fruit or flowers
Vegan sprinkles

1. Preheat the oven to 350 degrees F. Grease and flour three 8-inch cake pans.

2. In a medium bowl, whisk together the soy milk and apple cider vinegar. Allow the mixture to sit for at least 10 minutes so it can thicken and curdle.

3. In a large bowl, sift together the flour, baking powder, baking soda, and salt. Whisk to combine and set aside.

4. In the bowl of a stand mixer (or in a separate large bowl, using an electric hand mixer), cream together the sugar, vegan butter, and vanilla extract.

5. Run the mixer and slowly drizzle in the soured milk, beating to combine. Slowly add the flour mixture a little bit at a time and beat until combined.

6. Distribute the batter evenly among the prepared cake pans. Bake the cakes on the center rack of the oven for 27 to 30 minutes, until the cakes are golden and a toothpick inserted in the center comes out clean. Allow the cakes to cool in the pans. Carefully remove the cooled cakes from the pans.

(Continues)

7. When the cake layers have reached room temperature, you can frost and stack the cake layers. Do not frost before they have cooled completely, or your frosting will melt. If your cakes are a bit rounded at the top and you want them to be perfectly flat, use a cake leveler (or a sharp, serrated knife) to gently slice off the top of each cake, and flip them upside down for a perfectly level decorating surface. Spread or pipe a layer of frosting onto one layer of cake. Place the second cake on top and frost it. Repeat with the third cake. Then frost the top and sides of the cake.

8. Decorate with any additional toppings you like.

Friendly Suggestion: If you notice the cake frosting is softening or you won't be serving the cake immediately, store the cake in the refrigerator. The frosting will firm up in the fridge and the cake can last 5 days there.

Tester Tip: "I used two 9-inch pans and it worked great!" —Carol M.

My Tips

Buttercream Frosting

Frosting doesn't get any easier than this. With just three ingredients, you can whip up a batch in minutes. It works great on cakes, cupcakes, and even cookies. We encourage you to get colorful by playing with different frosting add-ins. You can use store-bought vegan food coloring, but one of my favorite discoveries was adding a little bit of defrosted frozen pink dragon fruit purée to this frosting, ½ teaspoon at a time, until I got the beautiful pink hue you see in the photo.

Yield: frosting for 12 cupcakes (about 2 cups)

Prep time: 15 minutes | Total time: 15 minutes

You'll need: an electric hand mixer

2 cups vegan butter, at room temperature (do not melt)
5½ cups powdered sugar
2 teaspoons vanilla extract
Coloring agent (optional)

1. Using an electric hand mixer, whip the vegan butter in a medium bowl until it's nice and smooth. Add the powdered sugar ½ cup at a time and mix until the mixture begins to have the consistency of frosting. Add the vanilla extract and whip until the frosting is smooth. If you'd like the frosting to be thicker, add additional powdered sugar a little bit at a time (and refrigerate to chill, which will make the frosting firm up).

2. If you'd like to color this frosting, add the coloring agent and mix well.

Friendly Suggestion: If you don't have time to let your butter come to room temp, it's better to use cold butter than to warm it in the microwave. Melted butter will not work for this frosting.

My Tips

Pumpkin Chocolate Pie

Want to play a fun game with your family at the dinner table? Ask them to guess the ingredients in this pie. They will never guess that what makes it smooth and creamy is . . . wait for it . . . *tofu*! Yep, filled with plant-based protein and puréed pumpkin, this pie is actually nutritious! This recipe is a great one for Thanksgiving—our families love it even more than a traditional pumpkin pie.

Yield: 8 servings

Prep time: 15 minutes | Cook time: 30 minutes | Total time: 8 hours and 45 minutes

You'll need: a blender

1 cup vegan semisweet chocolate chips
1 (15-ounce) can pure pumpkin purée (without added spices)
1½ cups silken (also called "soft") tofu, drained
1½ tablespoons packed brown sugar
1½ teaspoons vanilla extract
1½ tablespoons pumpkin pie spice
1 teaspoon ground cinnamon
1 prepared vegan piecrust
Vegan whipped cream (optional)

1. Preheat the oven to 350 degrees F.
2. In a small microwave-safe bowl, microwave the chocolate chips for 30 seconds. Mix with a fork until smooth. (If the chocolate is still lumpy, microwave for 20-second intervals, mixing in between, until the chocolate is completely smooth.)
3. In a blender, combine the pumpkin purée, tofu, brown sugar, vanilla extract, pumpkin pie spice, and cinnamon. Add the melted chocolate and blend on high until completely smooth.
4. Pour the pie filling into the prepared piecrust and bake for 30 minutes. The filling will not be fully set yet—that's okay! Remove from the oven and allow to cool in the pan.
5. Transfer the cooled pie to the refrigerator and let it set overnight or for at least 8 hours. Top with vegan whipped cream, if using.

My Tips

Grandma's Cookies

Ready to try the best cookies in the world? These are *technically* oatmeal cookies, but you'd never guess. They're nothing like those crumbly things you'd find in a health food store. Oh no, these chewy, almost toffee-like cookies make instant fans out of everyone who tries them. This recipe comes from my grandma's kitchen and has been passed down and veganized to perfection by my late birth father, Greg Hicks, whom we'll remember every time we eat these delicious cookies.

Yield: 24 cookies

Prep time: 20 minutes | Cook time: 12 minutes | Total time: 2 hours and 32 minutes

3 tablespoons ground flaxseed meal
½ cup water
1 cup vegetable shortening (such as Crisco)
2¼ cups packed light brown sugar
2 teaspoons vanilla extract
1½ cups all-purpose flour, sifted
1 teaspoon baking powder
1 teaspoon baking soda
1 teaspoon salt
3 cups old-fashioned rolled oats
1 cup powdered sugar

1. In a small ramekin, mix together the flaxseed meal and water. Set aside, allowing the mixture to rest and thicken for at least 10 minutes.
2. In a large bowl, beat the shortening and brown sugar together until thoroughly combined. Then stir in the vanilla extract and flaxseed meal mixture.
3. In a medium bowl, whisk together the flour, baking powder, baking soda, and salt.
4. Slowly add the flour mixture to the wet mixture and stir until well combined.
5. Mix in the rolled oats.
6. Using your hands, roll the dough into 1-inch balls. The dough will be sticky—don't worry, that's fine. You can rinse your hands with water as you work to help prevent the dough from sticking to your fingers and to make it easier to work with. Place the dough balls in containers or on a baking sheet (use parchment paper between layers of dough balls, if you're stacking), and refrigerate for at least 2 hours (or freeze until you're ready to bake).
7. When you're ready to bake, preheat the oven to 350 degrees F. Line a baking sheet with

parchment paper or a silicone mat. Pour the powdered sugar into a small bowl. Roll each ball in the powdered sugar, place the balls 3 inches apart on the prepared baking sheet, and flatten them by pressing down with a flat-bottomed glass dipped in powdered sugar.

8. Bake for 10 to 12 minutes, until the cookies are puffy and golden around the edges. The exact baking time depends on the size of your cookies. Allow them to cool on the pan for at least 15 minutes before enjoying (they should flatten and caramelize soon after you remove them from the oven).

Meal Planning Tip: If you like to plan ahead, you can make this cookie dough, roll it into balls, and freeze them for as long as you'd like (days, even weeks) until you're ready to bake.

My Tips

Peanut Butter Cookies

If peanut butter sets your heart aflutter, you'll swoon for these cookies! They're great to bake for the holidays, to take to work, or to bring to a friend who needs a pick-me-up. They're meant to be a little chewy, so keep an eye on them as they bake so you can pull them out of the oven before they start to brown. Everyone's oven is a little different, so depending on yours and the size of your cookies, you may need to adjust the cooking time accordingly.

Yield: 24 cookies

Prep time: 30 minutes | Cook time: 14 minutes | Total time: 44 minutes

You'll need: an electric mixer

½ cup vegan butter, softened at room temperature

¾ cup packed light brown sugar

¼ cup granulated sugar, plus additional ¼ cup for topping

¾ cup crunchy peanut butter

¼ cup unsweetened applesauce

1 teaspoon vanilla extract

1½ cups all-purpose flour

½ teaspoon baking soda

½ teaspoon cornstarch

Up to 2 tablespoons plant-based milk (any variety)

1. Preheat the oven to 350 degrees F. Line baking sheets with parchment paper or a silicone mat.
2. In a large bowl, whip together the vegan butter, brown sugar, and granulated sugar with an electric mixer until light and fluffy.
3. Add the peanut butter, applesauce, and vanilla extract and mix until fully combined.
4. Sift in the flour, baking soda, and cornstarch and mix until combined.
5. If the mixture is too dry and crumbly, add 1 to 2 tablespoons of plant-based milk and mix until combined. The dough should be thick and should stick together like Play-Doh when you press it with your hands.
6. Pour ¼ cup of granulated sugar into a small bowl. Roll the dough into 1-inch balls and dip each into the sugar, rolling gently to fully coat. Place the balls 2 inches apart on the prepared baking sheet. Using a fork, press each ball twice to flatten slightly and create a crisscross design atop each cookie.
7. Bake for 12 to 14 minutes, making sure to remove the cookies from the oven before they've browned. Allow to cool to room temperature

on the baking sheet for 20 minutes before enjoying. The cookies will firm up once they've cooled to room temperature.

Tester Tip: "I like using chunky turbinado sugar instead of granulated sugar for added crunch!" —Heather B.

My Tips

Thumbprint Cookies

We love minimalist baking, so the fact that this recipe calls for just a few staple pantry ingredients makes it one of our favorites. It's also a fun project to do with kiddos. Use their little thumbs to make the cookie indent, and help them put a dollop of preserves in the middle. Food is fun!

Yield: 40 cookies

Prep time: 40 minutes | Cook time: 17 minutes | Total time: 57 minutes

You'll need: an electric mixer

1 cup vegan butter, at
   room temperature
⅔ cup granulated sugar
1 teaspoon almond
   extract
1 teaspoon vanilla extract
2 cups all-purpose flour
Up to 6 teaspoons water,
   if needed
½ cup fruit preserves (we
   like raspberry best, but
   any will work)

My Tips

1. Preheat the oven to 350 degrees F. Lightly grease baking sheets or line with parchment paper or a silicone mat.

2. In a large bowl, beat the vegan butter and sugar with an electric mixer until fluffy. Add the almond and vanilla extracts and beat to combine. Add the flour ½ cup at a time, beating until the dough is well mixed. This will create a crumbly-looking dough that you should be able to mold together with your hands. If the dough is too crumbly to hold together, add water 1 teaspoon at a time until a more pliable dough forms (it should still look slightly crumbly).

3. Fill a tablespoon (or similarly sized cookie scoop) with dough, flattening the dough on top. Using your finger, push out the dough, domed side up, and place it on the prepared baking sheet. Repeat with the remaining dough, spacing the dough pieces 1 inch apart. Using the back of a teaspoon, make a small dent in the middle of each dome of cookie dough. Spoon 1 teaspoon of preserves into the dent on each cookie.

4. Bake for 16 to 17 minutes. Allow to cool on the pan for 30 minutes.

Fudgy Brownies

Brownies should be easy to make, but they're notoriously challenging to veganize. We went through many, many batches of brownies until we landed on these—our most chocolaty, chewy brownies of all. Make them the night before so they have a chance to chill in the fridge, and you'll be rewarded with the most fudgy brownies you've ever tasted.

Yield: 15 brownies

Prep time: 15 minutes | Cook time: 45 minutes | Total time: 1 hour (up to overnight)

¼ cup ground flaxseed meal

½ cup plus 2 tablespoons soy milk (any variety)

1 tablespoon vanilla extract

2 cups granulated sugar

1 cup all-purpose flour

1 cup cocoa powder

¼ teaspoon salt

1 teaspoon baking powder

¼ cup plus 1 tablespoon canola oil

¼ cup vegan semisweet chocolate chips, for topping

1. Preheat the oven to 350 degrees F. Line a 9 x 9-inch baking pan with parchment paper.

2. In a small bowl, mix together the ground flaxseed meal, soy milk, and vanilla extract. Set aside for at least 10 minutes to allow the mixture to thicken.

3. In a large bowl, combine the sugar, flour, cocoa powder, salt, and baking powder and whisk until well mixed.

4. Add the flaxseed meal mixture and canola oil to the dry ingredients and mix just until combined. Do not overmix.

5. Spoon the thick brownie batter into the prepared baking dish. Sprinkle the top evenly with the chocolate chips.

6. Bake for 45 minutes. Allow to cool fully in the pan. For the fudgiest texture, refrigerate overnight or for at least 4 hours before slicing and serving.

Friendly Suggestion: Yes, you can dive into these right out of the oven. But these brownies are best when enjoyed chilled, straight out of the fridge.

My Tips

Donuts

Is there anyone on Earth who doesn't love donuts? Well, now you can make them right at home, using fully plant-based ingredients, in less than an hour. These donuts are soft and fluffy and come out perfect every time. Once cooled, they can be dipped, drizzled, and sprinkled with any number of creative glazes and toppings. Below, we've included two of our favorite glazes: chocolate and maple cinnamon. If you want to get fancy, you can prep half a batch of each glaze and make two-toned donuts.

Yield: 10 donuts

Prep time: 20 minutes | Cook time: 19 minutes | Total time: 39 minutes

You'll need: a standard-sized nonstick donut pan

1½ cups vanilla soy milk (any variety)
2 tablespoons ground flaxseed meal
6 tablespoons canola oil
1 teaspoon vanilla extract
2 cups all-purpose flour
1 cup granulated sugar
1 tablespoon baking powder
¼ teaspoon salt

Classic Chocolate Glaze:

1 cup vegan chocolate chips, melted
1 teaspoon coconut oil (refined or unrefined), melted

Maple Cinnamon Glaze:

1½ cups powdered sugar
¼ cup pure maple syrup
1 teaspoon vanilla extract
1½ tablespoons water
3 pinches ground cinnamon

Optional Toppings:

Vegan sprinkles
Shredded coconut
Contrasting glaze to drizzle on top (see Friendly Suggestion below)

1. Preheat the oven to 350 degrees F. Grease your donut pan well.
2. In a small bowl, whisk together the soy milk, flaxseed meal, canola oil, and vanilla extract. Set aside for at least 5 minutes.
3. In a large bowl, combine the flour, sugar, baking powder, and salt and mix well.
4. Pour the wet mixture into the dry mixture and stir just until combined.
5. Spoon the batter evenly into the prepared donut pan, filling 10 donut molds partway (about three-quarters full). Do not fill them all the way to the top—doing so could cause the holes of the donuts to close up.
6. Bake for 17 to 19 minutes, until a toothpick inserted in the center comes out clean. Allow the donuts to cool in the pan, then pop the donuts out upside

down onto a cooling rack with parchment paper beneath it (which will catch the frosting drips).

7. Prepare your desired glaze by whisking together the glaze ingredients in a medium bowl.

8. Once the donuts have completely cooled to room temperature (we repeat: do not glaze the donuts before they have fully cooled!), dip each donut into the glaze to generously coat the top and some of the sides. Lift the donut out of the glaze, flip it over, and set it back on the cooling rack, allowing the glaze to drip down the sides and harden. Sprinkle with any optional toppings and allow the glaze to set completely. If you'd like the glaze to harden faster, place the donuts in the refrigerator.

Friendly Suggestion: Want to create a double-glaze drizzle effect? First, prepare two contrasting glazes (such as chocolate and maple). Dip the donut in the primary glaze, set it on the cooling rack, and use a spoon to drizzle on the secondary glaze.

Tester Tip: "I used this batter to make mini-donuts and simply adjusted the baking time to 12 minutes. They were delicious!" —Melissa B.

My Tips

Ice Cream Cake

 I love, love, love my mother-in-law, Jolene Shapiro, and this recipe comes from her kitchen. Once you've become familiar with the process of making this cake, she encourages you to play with the recipe by switching up the ice cream flavors, using crumbled cookies or brownies instead of chopped nuts, and trying peanut butter sandwich cookies like Nutter Butters or another variety instead of chocolate cookies. You can decorate this cake with piped Chocolate Frosting (page 169) or Buttercream Frosting (page 175), rainbow sprinkles, candy, fruit, cookies, a chocolate drizzle, and beyond.

Yield: 8 servings

Prep time: 30 minutes | Total time: 12 hours and 30 minutes

You'll need: a food processor and a springform pan (8 inches wide × 3½ inches deep)

2 (1-pint) containers vegan vanilla ice cream

2 (1-pint) containers vegan ice cream in a flavor other than vanilla (they should be the same flavor)

1 (14.3-ounce) package chocolate sandwich cookies (such as Oreos)

½ cup vegan butter, at room temperature

2 cups chopped peanuts (or another package of cookies that you can lay flat for the middle layer), divided

Optional Decorations:

Melted chocolate, Chocolate Shell (page 195), or Classic Chocolate Glaze (page 189), cooled

Vegan rainbow sprinkles

Chocolate Frosting (page 169)

Buttercream Frosting (page 175)

Chopped peanuts

Fruit

1. Take the ice cream out of the refrigerator and allow it to thaw on the counter while you prepare the crust.

2. In the bowl of a food processor, combine the whole package of cookies and the vegan butter. Process until thoroughly combined.

3. Line a springform pan (8 inches wide × 3½ inches deep) with parchment paper. To do so, cut one piece of parchment to the size of the bottom of the pan, and cut another strip to wrap around the sides.

4. Using your hands, evenly press the cookie mixture into a thin layer on the bottom of the pan. (This will leave the sides of the cake exposed so you can see the layers, but if you're worried about the ice cream melting, you can press the cookie mixture up the sides of the pan, too, for a crust that will keep the ice cream well contained while serving.)

5. Scoop the vanilla ice cream out of the cartons and spread it into an even layer over the cookie mixture.
6. Evenly spread 2 cups of the chopped peanuts (or sandwich cookies laid flat) over the vanilla ice cream.
7. Scoop the other-flavored ice cream over the peanuts and spread it into an even layer. (If you added cookie mixture to the sides of your pan and there is any excess reaching above the sides of the ice cream, cut the excess away so the cookie mixture is level with the ice cream cake.) Lay a piece of parchment paper over the open top of the springform pan, and press the parchment against the ice cream until it's tightly packed.
8. Place the ice cream cake in the freezer and allow it to harden overnight or for at least 12 hours.
9. Remove the ice cream cake from the freezer, invert it onto a plate, and undo the springform pan. Flip the cake onto a serving plate or cake stand.
10. Top the cake with any of the optional decorations. Serve the cake immediately or return it to the freezer until you are ready to serve.

Tester Tip: "If presentation is important and you want clean lines, then pop the bottom layer of vanilla ice cream back into the freezer to firm up before adding the next layer of ice cream on top." —Emily R.

My Tips

_____

_____

_____

My Tips

Banana Nice Cream Sundae

If you've been on Instagram in the last few years, you've probably discovered the wonders of "banana nice cream"—one-ingredient soft serve made simply from blended frozen bananas. It's incredibly tasty and easy to prepare, and we still can't believe it's actually healthy.

Yield: 2–3 servings

Prep time: 15 minutes | Total time: 15 minutes | Advance prep required (freeze the bananas)

You'll need: a food processor

Chocolate Shell:

3 tablespoons vegan chocolate chips

1 tablespoon coconut oil (refined or unrefined)

Nice Cream:

4 large, spotty, ripe bananas, peeled, sliced, and frozen for at least 24 hours

¼ cup cocoa powder (optional)

2 tablespoons peanut butter (any type) (optional)

Optional Toppings:

Chopped peanuts
Vegan rainbow sprinkles
Vegan whipped cream
Cherries

1. To make the chocolate shell, in a small microwave-safe ramekin, combine the chocolate chips and coconut oil. Melt in the microwave, heating for 20-second increments and mixing with a spoon between each, until a smooth chocolate sauce forms.

2. To make the nice cream, place the frozen bananas in the bowl of a food processor. Add the cocoa powder and peanut butter (if using them). Process on high, pausing to push down the sides as needed, until the mixture has the creamy, soft texture of ice cream. Do not add liquid. The bananas will get crumbly at first, but be patient— the mixture will become creamy.

3. Scoop into bowls and drizzle with the chocolate shell (it will harden when it's added to the cold nice cream). Top with any optional toppings. Serve immediately.

Friendly Suggestion: If you don't have a food processor, you can make this in a blender. You may need to add a splash of plant-based milk to get things moving and will likely need to stop and push the bananas down several times before the mixture starts developing the texture of ice cream.

Chocolate Peanut Butter Milkshake

What if we told you that you could have a thick, creamy chocolate shake that's actually *good* for you? Well, you can! This milkshake is made with a base of frozen bananas and protein-packed peanut butter. It is decadent, for sure, but boasts healthy fruit, fiber, and antioxidants, too. This recipe makes enough for two servings.

As always, we encourage you to mix it up! Prefer a vanilla shake? Omit the cocoa powder and peanut butter and use vanilla soy milk. Want a peanut butter shake? Skip the cocoa powder. Craving a creamy strawberry milkshake? Drop the cocoa and PB and add some fresh or frozen strawberries. The sky really is the limit with this one.

Yield: 1 large shake or 2 small shakes

Prep time: 5 minutes | Total time: 5 minutes

You'll need: a high-powered blender

Advance prep required (freeze the bananas)

2 large super-ripe bananas, peeled, sliced, and frozen for at least 6 hours

1 cup soy milk (any variety)

¼ cup cocoa powder

2 heaping tablespoons peanut butter (any type)

In a high-powered blender, blend all the ingredients until creamy. Depending on your blender, it may take a little patience to get things moving (pause and push the ingredients down with a spoon before resuming, repeating as needed). It will be worth it!

Why It Works: The frozen bananas are what create the super-thick milkshake-like consistency, so make sure your bananas are completely frozen before blending.

My Tips

Chocolate Mousse

This is one of the all-time easiest and most versatile chocolate mousse recipes. It's inspired by the chocolate pie in Toni's second cookbook, *Plant-Based on a Budget*. Not only is this dessert super quick to make, but it's also loaded with protein. Win-win!

   This mousse also forms the base of our decadent Fudge Pops (page 200)—so if you make a batch and freeze some in popsicle molds, you can enjoy it two ways.

Yield: 4–6 servings

Prep time: 15 minutes | Total time: 45 minutes

You'll need: a blender or food processor

1 (12-ounce) bag vegan semisweet chocolate chips

1 (14-ounce) block silken (also called "soft") tofu, drained

2 teaspoons vanilla extract

4–6 raspberries, for topping

Optional Toppings:

4 sprigs mint

Vegan whipped cream

Shaved vegan chocolate

1. Melt the chocolate using a microwave or double boiler (see the box on page 19 for chocolate melting instructions).

2. In a blender or food processor, blend the melted chocolate, tofu, and vanilla extract until creamy.

3. Pour the tofu-chocolate mixture into 4 to 6 small ramekins and refrigerate for 30 minutes or until the filling solidifies. Top with raspberries and any optional toppings.

My Tips

Fudge Pops

This recipe is a spin-off of one that made its debut in Toni's second cookbook, *Plant-Based on a Budget*, in the shape of a chocolate pie. The filling was so good that we thought, "Hey, we wonder how these would do in popsicle molds." And we're glad we tried it, because they're A-M-A-Z-I-N-G! Can't wait for the creamy mixture to freeze into popsicles? You can also enjoy this without the wait as Chocolate Mousse (page 199).

Yield: 6–9 pops

Prep time: 15 minutes | Total time: 8 hours and 15 minutes

You'll need: a blender or food processor and popsicle molds

1 (12-ounce) bag vegan semisweet chocolate chips

1 (14-ounce) block silken (also called "soft") tofu, drained

2 teaspoons vanilla extract

1. In a small microwave-safe bowl, microwave the chocolate chips for 45 seconds. Mix with a fork until smooth. If the chocolate is still lumpy, microwave in additional 20-second intervals, stirring in between, until the chocolate is completely smooth. Alternatively, use a double boiler to melt the chocolate (see the box on page 19).

2. In a blender or food processor, blend the melted chocolate, tofu, and vanilla extract until creamy.

3. Pour the tofu-chocolate mixture into popsicle molds and place in the freezer overnight or for at least 8 hours.

Friendly Suggestion: If the fudge pops don't easily pop out of their molds, run them under warm water to loosen them.

Tester Tip: "Want to add fun fillings to your fudge pops? After step 2, chill the fudge pop mix in the fridge until it forms up. Then add it to your popsicle mold, create a center, add fruit preserves or peanut butter, and return to the freezer. These flavors nicely complement the fudge!"—Michelle R.

My Tips

Chia Pudding Parfait

If you're a lover of tapioca or rice pudding, you're going to love this healthful spin. When combined with a liquid, chia seeds develop a consistency like tapioca pearls, which gives the pudding a nostalgic texture. Plus, chia pudding is way easier to make (no cooking required!) and it's loaded with nutrients, including omega-3s. Not just an evening treat, it doubles as an all-star make-ahead breakfast that can be topped with fresh fruit, granola, or whatever strikes your fancy (see our favorite topping suggestions below).

Yield: 2–3 servings

Prep time: 5 minutes | Total time: 12 hours

¾ cup unsweetened, plain soy milk
¼ cup chia seeds
½ teaspoon vanilla extract
1 tablespoon maple syrup

Optional Toppings:

Strawberry Preserves (page 245)
Granola (store-bought or from the recipe on page 46)
Fresh berries or sliced fruit
Sliced almonds
Shredded coconut
Vegan whipped cream
Sprig of mint

1. In a jar, bowl, or container, combine the soy milk, chia seeds, vanilla extract, and maple syrup. Mix well until combined, ensuring that there are no clumps of chia seeds. The seeds will separate from the milk—that's okay. Cover and place in the refrigerator overnight or for at least 12 hours, stirring midway to break up the chia again.

2. Divide the set pudding into small ramekins (it's filling!) and top with any optional toppings.

My Tips

Meal Planning Tip: When refrigerated, this chia pudding will keep its freshness for at least 5 days, so it's a great make-ahead dessert if you have guests coming over and don't want to do all the cooking on that day.

Tester Tip: "I love this with 1 to 2 tablespoons of cocoa powder mixed in and topped with some mini vegan chocolate chips!"—Melanie S.

Fudge

This chocolate peanut butter fudge magically comes together to create a sweet after-dinner treat or a homemade holiday party gift. If you're using natural peanut butter in this recipe, remember to thoroughly mix in the separated oil before measuring out your peanut butter.

Yield: 20+ servings

Prep time: 20 minutes | Total time: 4 hours and 20 minutes

½ cup refined coconut oil
½ cup unsweetened creamy peanut butter
1 tablespoon soy milk (any variety)
¼ cup cocoa powder
½ teaspoon vanilla extract
Pinch of salt
2 cups powdered sugar

Optional Toppings:

Chopped nuts
Shredded coconut
Vegan chocolate chips

1. Line a medium container (such as a 6 × 8-inch food storage container) with parchment paper.

2. In a large microwave-safe glass bowl, combine the coconut oil, peanut butter, and soy milk. Microwave for 30 seconds or until melted. Remove from the microwave and whisk together by hand until thoroughly combined.

3. Add the cocoa powder, vanilla extract, and salt and stir well with a spoon. Slowly add the powdered sugar while mixing until a thick dough forms.

4. Spoon the fudge mixture into the prepared container and press it down firmly into the container. Using an extra piece of parchment paper, cover the top and press on the parchment with your hands to smooth down the fudge. Discard the extra piece of parchment.

5. Top with any optional toppings, cover, and refrigerate for at least 4 hours or until ready to enjoy.

Friendly Suggestion: Refined coconut oil doesn't have a coconut flavor like unrefined coconut oil does, which is why we chose it for this recipe. But if you like a strong coconut taste, you can substitute unrefined coconut oil.

Why It Works: Coconut oil is solid at room temperature and liquid when warm. That's what helps this fudge come together seamlessly and then firm up in the fridge.

Peanut Butter Cups

Prepping for a Halloween party? Want to surprise your coworkers with a sweet treat? Or do you simply need to treat yourself? Whatever the reason or season, these peanut butter cups are waiting for you. With just three ingredients you probably have in your kitchen already, you can bring these homemade nuggets of chocolaty heaven to life. Sharing is optional.

Yield: 12 peanut butter cups

Prep time: 20 minutes | Total time: 1 hour and 20 minutes

½ cup creamy peanut butter
2 tablespoons powdered sugar
1 (12-ounce) bag vegan chocolate chips

1. Line a muffin pan with paper or silicone liners.
2. In a small bowl, combine the peanut butter and powdered sugar and mix well.
3. Place the chocolate chips in a small microwave-safe bowl and melt in the microwave for 45 seconds. Stir and continue to heat in 20-second increments until the chocolate is smooth when stirred. Alternatively, use a double boiler to melt the chocolate (see instructions below). Be careful not to burn the chocolate (which will make it seize and clump up irreversibly).
4. Using a spoon, spread a thin layer of melted chocolate on the bottom of each cupcake liner. Add 1 heaping teaspoon of peanut butter mixture in the center and gently spread it out a little with your finger. Cover the peanut butter with a small amount of additional chocolate, using your finger to swirl it around the top to cover the peanut butter completely.
5. Refrigerate the peanut butter cups for at least 1 hour or until the chocolate has hardened. Remove the peanut butter cups from the cupcake liners and store in the fridge for up to 2 weeks.

My Tips

Drinks

Whether you want to warm up with a cozy beverage on a cold winter's day or cool yourself off with a refreshing elixir in the heat of summer, you'll find a drink for every occasion in this chapter.

Save money with our homemade Pumpkin Spice Latte (page 210), visit the tropics without leaving home with our Virgin Piña Colada (page 221), and wow guests with our Eggnog (page 217) made *without eggs*.

Pumpkin Spice Latte

This recipe is for all the PSL lovers out there. It's sweet and simple and spiced with the best flavors of fall. Plus, if you make this at home instead of shelling out your hard-earned dollars at the cafe, you'll save *tons* of moolah. Made with sweetened soy milk (*not* the unsweetened or low-fat variety, please!), this recipe produces one decadent latte. If you're making it for two people, simply double the batch. And if you're wondering what to do with the extra pumpkin purée, you can freeze it (see Love Your Leftovers below).

Yield: 1 serving

Cook time: 10 minutes | Total time: 10 minutes

1 cup vanilla soy milk (the regular, sweetened kind)
2 tablespoons plus ½ teaspoon canned pure pumpkin purée (without added spices)
1½ tablespoons packed brown sugar
¾ teaspoon pumpkin pie spice, plus an optional dash for sprinkling
Pinch of salt
½ cup strong freshly brewed coffee
Vegan whipped cream (optional)

1. In a small pot over medium heat, combine the soy milk, pumpkin purée, brown sugar, pumpkin pie spice, and salt and whisk vigorously. Turn the heat off as soon as the mixture starts to boil.

2. In your favorite mug, combine the hot coffee and the milk mixture. Top with vegan whipped cream and sprinkle with pumpkin pie spice (if using them).

Love Your Leftovers: You can use an ice cube tray to premeasure the remaining pumpkin purée and freeze it to use for your future PSLs. For extra efficiency, add premeasured amounts of brown sugar, pumpkin pie spice, and salt to each cube of pumpkin purée and freeze these all together, so you can just pop a frozen spiced pumpkin cube into the pot with soy milk when you want a latte.

My Tips

Mexican Hot Chocolate

 I grew up drinking Ibarra hot chocolate and love my memories of my grandma breaking a triangular wedge from the chocolate wheel to boil with warm milk. This made-from-scratch vegan version takes me right back to my grandma's kitchen. The chocolate chips make this a rich and decadent treat, and the spices give it a boost of flavor that makes this drink perfect for the holidays or chilly winter nights. If you've never had chili powder in your hot cocoa before, prepare to fall in love.

Yield: 2 servings

Cook time: 10 minutes | Total time: 10 minutes

4 cups unsweetened, plain soy milk

½ cup plus 1 tablespoon vegan semisweet chocolate chips

2 teaspoons ground cinnamon

⅛ teaspoon chili powder

1½ teaspoons vanilla extract

½ teaspoon granulated sugar

Vegan whipped cream (optional)

1. In a medium pot over medium heat, warm the soy milk until it starts to boil. Stir in the chocolate chips and cook, stirring occasionally, until they fully melt, 5 to 7 minutes.

2. Whisk in the cinnamon, chili powder, vanilla extract, and sugar.

3. Serve hot topped with whipped cream (if using).

Friendly Suggestion: This tastes extra good topped with some vegan mini marshmallows (we love the Dandies brand).

> **My Tips**
>
> _____
>
> _____
>
> _____

Horchata

 Before I became vegan, I loved horchata. Anytime I dined at a Mexican restaurant, it was my go-to drink. My tía Lala (aka Aunt Laura) would always make a fresh pitcher when I visited as a kid, and I now have happy memories attached to it. Unfortunately, it's almost always made with cow's milk. But lucky for us, it's surprisingly easy to make this popular Mexican drink from scratch, without animal products. All you need are six ingredients and a little patience, and you've got a sweet, cinnamon-spiked rice milk beverage.

Yield: 4-6 servings (8 cups)

Prep time: 10 minutes | Total time: 4 hours and 10 minutes

You'll need: a high-powered blender and a nut milk bag or cheesecloth

1 cup uncooked long-grain white or brown rice

6 cups water, divided

½ cup granulated sugar

1½ tablespoons ground cinnamon

1½ teaspoons vanilla extract

2 cups unsweetened, plain plant-based milk

1. In a high-powered blender, combine the rice, 1½ cups of water, sugar, cinnamon, and vanilla extract, and blend until the rice is broken up and the water looks very milky. Don't worry, this won't harm your blender.

2. Pour the mixture into a pitcher, add the remaining 4½ cups of water and the milk, and stir. Let the mixture sit in the refrigerator overnight—or for at least 4 hours (the longer it sits, the more milky it will taste).

3. Pour the horchata into another pitcher (or large bowl), using a nut milk bag or cheesecloth to strain out the rice pulp. Discard the rice pulp.

4. Whisk the horchata thoroughly and serve cold, over ice.

My Tips

Eggnog

Holiday nog holds a special place in our hearts. For many, it is the epitome of Christmas and brings back memories of holiday parties through the years. Well, don't worry, dear friends. Just because you're avoiding eggs doesn't mean you have to forgo your favorite holiday drink. Using the magic of cashews and coconut cream, we've re-created a holiday nog that is every bit as luscious as the nog you grew up drinking, and redolent of the cozy flavors of winter.

Yield: 4–6 servings

Prep time: 10 minutes | Total time: 7 hours

You'll need: a high-powered blender

Advance prep required (soak the cashews)

½ cup raw cashews, soaked in water overnight or for at least 4 hours, drained, and rinsed

1 cup water

1 cup full-fat coconut cream

1 cup unsweetened, plain soy milk

2½ tablespoons granulated sugar

1½ teaspoons vanilla extract

1 teaspoon ground cinnamon

¼ teaspoon ground nutmeg

⅛ teaspoon ground cloves

⅛ teaspoon ground cardamom

1. In a high-powered blender, combine the soaked cashews, water, coconut cream, soy milk, sugar, vanilla extract, cinnamon, nutmeg, cloves, and cardamom and purée until smooth.

2. Place the nog in the refrigerator and chill for 2 to 3 hours. Stir the nog and serve cold.

My Tips

Pink Lemonade

There are few drinks as simple, fun, and refreshing as pink lemonade. During our rigorous recipe testing, we discovered that individual lemonade preferences vary—*a lot*. Some like it super sweet, others prefer theirs extra lemony with a big tart punch, while others like a less intense, more diluted flavor. Ours is tart and tangy, but you can easily adjust it to suit your palate. If you'd like it sweeter, add more sugar. If it's too potent, add more water. Prefer a pinker hue? Add an extra splash of cranberry juice (just a little at a time because the color changes fast).

Yield: 4–6 servings

Prep time: 15 minutes | Total time: 15 minutes

½ cup room-temperature water
1 cup granulated sugar
4 cups cold water
2½ cups freshly squeezed lemon juice
2 generous pinches of salt
1–2 tablespoons pure cranberry juice (adjust to achieve desired pink color)

1. In a small saucepan, bring ½ cup of room-temperature water to a boil over medium heat. Add the sugar and whisk until dissolved to create a simple syrup, about 3 minutes. Remove from the heat.

2. In a pitcher, combine 4 cups of cold water with the lemon juice, simple syrup, and salt and mix well. Slowly add the cranberry juice (just a little bit at a time) until you achieve your desired hue of pink. Note that a small amount of pure cranberry juice will change the color dramatically. (If using diluted cranberry juice rather than pure cranberry juice, you'll need more.)

Friendly Suggestion: Can't find pure cranberry juice? Other forms of cranberry juice will work too—you'll just need to adjust the amount you add to get your desired pink hue.

My Tips

Virgin Piña Colada

This tropical mocktail reminds us of getting caught in the rain, and fun times on sunny, sandy beaches. If you really want to kick up the festive summertime vibes, pop on some Hawaiian tunes, throw a mini umbrella into your glass, and have yourself a tiki night.

Yield: 2 servings

Prep time: 10 minutes | Total time: 10 minutes

You'll need: a blender

1 cup pineapple juice
2 cups frozen pineapple
¾ cup coconut cream
(full-fat coconut milk
from a can will also
work—just be sure to
shake the can before
opening)
1 cup ice
Pineapple slices, for
garnish (optional)

1. In a blender, combine the pineapple juice, frozen pineapple, coconut cream, and ice and pulse until smooth.
2. Serve immediately in two tall glasses. Garnish with pineapple slices (if using).

My Tips

DIY Staples

Cooking from scratch saves a lot of money, and because you're not relying on packaged foods, it's more eco-friendly, too. In this chapter, you'll learn to make your own pizza crust, breads, dressings, sauces, and more. We also love making our own nut milk (see Almond Milk on page 224).

Three of our absolute favorites are our homemade Pesto (page 227), which can be used on pasta, crostini, sandwiches, and wraps; our Marinara Sauce (page 228), which will take your pasta to another level; and our Mushroom Gravy (page 231), which is always a big hit at the holidays. Enjoy!

Almond Milk

Making your own milk is a great way to reduce packaging waste (you can buy the raw nuts from bulk bins), save money, and eliminate the additives commonly found in store-bought milks. Once you get in the habit of making your own milk from scratch, you'll never need to buy it again.

This makes a pretty creamy almond milk. If you like yours even creamier, reduce the amount of water, and if you like it lighter, reduce the amount of almonds (or add more water). Adjust the flavors and sweetener to your preference, and feel free to add 1 or 2 tablespoons of cocoa powder for chocolate milk. If you'll be using this in savory recipes, simply omit the sugar and vanilla extract.

Yield: 4–6 servings (4+ cups)

Prep time: 15 minutes | Total time: 12 hours

You'll need: a high-powered blender and a nut milk bag

Advance prep required (soak the almonds)

1 cup raw almonds, soaked in water overnight or for at least 4 hours, drained, and rinsed
4 cups water, divided
1 tablespoon granulated sugar
1 teaspoon vanilla extract

My Tips

1. In a high-powered blender, combine the almonds and 2 cups of water and blend on high until smooth. Add the remaining 2 cups of water, sugar, and vanilla extract and blend again until smooth. There is no risk of overblending, so don't worry about blending too long.

2. Hold your nut milk bag open over a large bowl and pour the nut milk mixture into the bag. The milk will pass through the bag while the pulp remains. Using your hands, squeeze the nut milk bag until all the liquid has passed through and only the crumbly fibrous pulp remains. Discard the pulp.

3. Transfer the nut milk to a large mason jar or other container with a tight seal. Store in the refrigerator and use within 5 days.

Friendly Suggestion: Instead of sugar, try fresh Medjool dates, maple syrup, or agave to sweeten your milk.

Pesto

This nutty, herbaceous pesto is made with walnuts instead of pine nuts, which will save you *tons* of money, and we promise you won't even notice the difference. It's *that* good! With just six ingredients, this versatile and flavorful spread/dip/sauce is great on pizza (page 100), pasta (page 81), and crostini (page 147).

Yield: 2 cups

Prep time: 5 minutes | Total time: 5 minutes

You'll need: a high-powered blender or food processor

½ cup tightly packed
    fresh basil leaves
1 cup raw walnuts
1 teaspoon minced garlic
    (from about 2 small
    cloves)
½ cup olive oil
2 tablespoons nutritional
    yeast
1 teaspoon salt

In a high-powered blender or food processor, combine all the ingredients and blend on high until smooth and creamy. Enjoy the pesto immediately or store in a sealed jar in the fridge for up to 5 days.

My Tips

Marinara Sauce

This rustic pasta sauce tastes like a trip to Italy. Loaded with fresh garlic, onion, spices, and chunky tomatoes, it's the classic complement to spaghetti—or our favorite, capellini (angel-hair pasta). It's also divine with our Stuffed Shells (page 70) and Lasagna (page 60). Enjoy this sauce chunky, or blend it partially or fully with an immersion blender, which will transform it into a smoother marinara.

Yield: 3 cups

Prep time: 15 minutes | Cook time: 56 minutes | Total time: 1 hour and 11 minutes

¼ cup extra-virgin olive oil

1 small yellow onion, diced

6 medium cloves garlic, roughly chopped

1 teaspoon dried oregano

1 (28-ounce) can whole peeled tomatoes, with their juices

¾ teaspoon salt

½ teaspoon dried basil

¼ teaspoon red chili pepper flakes (optional if you don't do spice)

1. In a large skillet over medium-high heat, heat the olive oil. Add the onion and sauté for about 5 minutes, until softened and translucent. Add the garlic and oregano and sauté for 1 minute more.

2. Pour in the whole can of peeled tomatoes with their juices, then add the salt, basil, and red chili pepper flakes (if using). Lower the heat.

3. Simmer the sauce for 15 minutes. With the back of a wooden spoon, gently mash the whole tomatoes. You can cut them apart by pressing them against the side of the pan with the side of the spoon. Just be careful—their juices can pop!

4. Simmer the sauce for 30 minutes more to allow the flavors to meld. Enjoy immediately or cool and store in a sealed jar in the refrigerator for up to 5 days.

Friendly Suggestion: When serving with pasta, add salt and pepper to taste.

My Tips

Mushroom Gravy

Confession time: we are both die-hard mushroom haters. Yet somehow, magically, when we mince the mushrooms for this gravy, our aversion to fungi disappears! Whipping up a batch of this gravy will make your entire home smell like Thanksgiving, but you certainly don't have to wait for the holidays to make it. Goodness, no! We make this gravy year-round to pour over Mashed Potatoes (page 130). It's also an integral part of our Shepherd's Pie (page 69), which we pair with a fresh batch of Dinner Rolls (page 254).

Yield: 3 cups

Prep time: 15 minutes | Cook time: 20 minutes | Total time: 30 minutes

1 cup button mushrooms (you'll need about 5)
3½ tablespoons canola or vegetable oil
½ cup diced yellow onion
2 large cloves garlic, minced
2 bay leaves
3½ tablespoons all-purpose flour
2 cups vegetable broth (or equivalent amount of vegetable bouillon and water)
½ teaspoon dried oregano
Ground black pepper, to taste

1. Wash the mushrooms, remove the stems (if desired), and chop super finely.

2. Heat the oil in a saucepan over medium heat. Add the mushrooms, onion, garlic, and bay leaves. Sauté for 2 to 3 minutes, until the onion is translucent and tender. Remove the bay leaves.

3. Add the flour and mix to form a thick paste. Cook, stirring, for 1 to 2 minutes, until the sauce is golden.

4. Add the vegetable broth, stir, and bring to a simmer. Season with the oregano and pepper.

5. Use a whisk to gently mix the gravy occasionally until it thickens to your desired consistency, about 20 minutes. If you prefer a thinner gravy, mix in 1 to 2 tablespoons of water.

My Tips

BBQ Pulled Jackfruit

Have you ever tried jackfruit as a meat alternative? Tearing apart young green jackfruit (which you can find canned in many grocery stores) and cooking it up in your favorite barbecue sauce gives it a remarkably meaty texture and flavor that is crazy similar to that of pulled pork. But it's oh so much better for you. Our smoky, tangy jackfruit is deee-licious in our Jackfruit "Pulled Pork" Sandwich (page 88), in tacos, over our Mac 'n' Cheese (page 63), over chips with Nacho Cheese Sauce (page 137), and anywhere else you'd use barbecued pulled pork.

Yield: 4 servings

Prep time: 20 minutes | Cook time: 10 minutes | Total time: 30 minutes

2 (20-ounce) cans young green jackfruit, drained

1 tablespoon canola or vegetable oil

½ small red onion, diced

2 medium cloves garlic, minced

1 teaspoon smoked paprika

1 cup vegan barbecue sauce (store-bought or from the recipe on page 237)

1. Using your fingers, pull apart the jackfruit pieces into shreds and remove all the tough pieces. Place the shreds and the oil in a medium pan.

2. Place the pan over medium-high heat and add the onion and garlic. Sauté for 4 minutes or until the onion becomes translucent. Add the paprika and cook for 3 more minutes.

3. Pour in the barbecue sauce and cook for 3 minutes. Serve hot.

Love Your Leftovers: The barbecue jackfruit can be refrigerated and reheats nicely, so you can double this recipe for easy meal planning or simply to enjoy more leftovers. We promise, it's so good you're going to want more tomorrow.

My Tips

Tofu Bacon

We make our own bacon out of one of our most beloved staples: tofu. When baked together with our special smoky bacon marinade, the tofu becomes reminiscent of traditional bacon—but without harming a soul.

Yield: 9 pieces of tofu bacon

Prep time: 8 minutes | Cook time: 30 minutes | Total time: 38 minutes

1 tablespoon canola or vegetable oil

1 (16-ounce block) extra-firm tofu, pressed (we highly recommend vacuum-sealed tofu)

2 tablespoons soy sauce

1 tablespoon water

1 tablespoon pure maple syrup

½ tablespoon liquid smoke

1. Preheat the oven to 400 degrees F. Coat a 9 × 9-inch baking pan with the oil.

2. Cut the tofu block in half lengthwise (you will be using only half, so return the other portion to the fridge to use in another recipe). Cut the tofu lengthwise into thin strips about ⅛ inch thick, or as thinly as possible. Optionally, you may then cut these strips in half lengthwise. Place the tofu in the prepared pan and bake for 10 minutes. Flip and bake for 5 more minutes.

3. While the tofu is baking, in a small bowl, combine the soy sauce, water, maple syrup, and liquid smoke.

4. Remove the pan from the oven and pour the liquid blend over the tofu. Return the tofu to the oven, bake for 10 minutes, flip, and bake for 5 more minutes. Allow to cool for 5 minutes.

My Tips

_____

_____

_____

Marinated Tofu

Tofu on its own is rather bland, but it's that inherent absence of flavor that makes it so adaptable to different marinades and sauces. The longer the tofu marinates, the more flavorful it will become. At minimum, marinate the tofu overnight, but if possible, a full day or even two is ideal. That's it! Now you're ready to bake, grill, fry, and devour these three varieties of marinated tofu.

Yield: 4–6 servings

Prep time: 10 minutes | Cook time: 40 minutes | Total time: 8 hours 50 minutes

1 (16-ounce) block extra-firm tofu

1 batch marinade (such as Orange Ginger Marinade, page 241; Teriyaki Sauce, page 240; or Barbecue Sauce, page 237)

1. Press the tofu.
2. Cut the tofu into ¼- to ½-inch-thick slices. Proceed with the recipe according to which sauce or marinade you chose.

To marinate and bake:

3. Using a toothpick, stab the tofu in several places to enable the marinade to seep more deeply into the tofu.
4. Place the tofu pieces in a casserole dish or tall-rimmed pan and cover with your marinade of choice. Place in the refrigerator and marinate for at least 8 hours. (We like to let it sit overnight for a richer taste.)
5. Preheat the oven to 350 degrees F.
6. Once the tofu is marinated, pour out a portion of the marinade so that the tofu is only halfway submerged.
7. Bake for about 40 minutes, until the tofu turns a golden brown.

(Continues)

To bake tofu with thick sauces (such as teriyaki or barbecue):

3. Place the sliced tofu in a large casserole dish. Pour your sauce of choice over the tofu until all pieces are fully submerged. Let the tofu sit for at least 30 minutes.
4. Preheat the oven to 350 degrees F. Line a rimmed baking sheet with parchment paper or a silicone mat.
5. Using a spatula, transfer the tofu to the prepared baking sheet. Brush extra sauce on each piece of tofu. Bake for 20 minutes.
6. Remove from the oven, flip each piece, brush with the sauce in the pan, and bake for another 20 minutes.

My Tips

Barbecue Sauce

This barbecue sauce has clean ingredients and tastes great on our BBQ Pizza (page 99), BBQ Pulled Jackfruit (page 232), and atop our Black Bean Burgers (page 87).

Yield: 2 cups

Prep time: 10 minutes | Cook time: 10 minutes | Total time: 20 minutes

1½ cups ketchup
½ cup apple cider vinegar
¼ cup packed brown sugar
2 tablespoons yellow mustard
2 tablespoons vegan Worcestershire sauce
2½ teaspoons smoked paprika
1 teaspoon onion powder
½ teaspoon garlic powder
¼ teaspoon ground black pepper
¼ teaspoon salt

In a saucepan over medium-low heat, stir together all the ingredients. Lower the heat and simmer for 10 minutes. Remove from the heat. Use the sauce immediately or cool it and store it in a sealed jar in the fridge for up to 1 week.

My Tips

Thousand Island Dressing

Our popular Thousand Island dressing is loved by many for its flavor and versatility. It's a fantastic dipping sauce, a delicious burger spread, and a familiar salad topping, but whichever way you use it, it's bound to be tasty.

This recipe doesn't require anything fancy—just a knife, a bowl, a spoon, and simple ingredients that you mix together to create magic. This dressing's flavor improves with time, so you can prepare a batch and store it in the fridge, allowing the flavors to marry.

Yield: 1 cup

Prep time: 10 minutes | Total time: 10 minutes

½ cup vegan mayo
2½ tablespoons ketchup
2½ tablespoons sweet relish
1 tablespoon minced red onion
½ teaspoon garlic powder
1 teaspoon lemon juice
⅛ teaspoon salt

In a medium bowl, combine all the ingredients and mix thoroughly. Use the dressing immediately or store it in a glass jar in the fridge for up to 1 week.

My Tips

Teriyaki Sauce

Skip the store-bought bottle and go with our flavorful teriyaki sauce. You can use it in Marinated Tofu (page 235), add a tablespoon to our Tofu Scramble (page 22) for extra flavor, or use it to whip up a stir-fry.

Yield: 1½ cups

Prep time: 15 minutes | Cook time: 5 minutes | Total time: 20 minutes

1¼ cups water, divided
½ cup soy sauce
¼ cup plus 1 tablespoon packed brown sugar
1 tablespoon maple syrup
1 teaspoon minced fresh ginger
2 small cloves garlic, minced
½ teaspoon ground ginger
½ teaspoon garlic powder
½ teaspoon apple cider vinegar
2 tablespoons cornstarch

1. In a medium pot, whisk together 1 cup of water and the soy sauce, brown sugar, maple syrup, fresh ginger, fresh garlic, ground ginger, garlic powder, and apple cider vinegar.
2. In a small bowl, whisk together the cornstarch and the remaining ¼ cup of water. Add the mixture to the pot.
3. Place the pot over high heat and whisk while bringing to a boil, allowing the sauce to boil for 5 minutes while whisking frequently. Remove from the heat. Use the sauce immediately or pour it into a glass jar and store it in the fridge for up to 5 days.

Friendly Suggestion: You can change the consistency of the teriyaki sauce by varying the cooking time, boiling for less than 5 minutes for a thinner sauce, or more than 5 minutes for a thicker sauce.

My Tips

Orange Ginger Marinade

This simple marinade packs a punch of flavor with a marriage of sweet, salty, and acidic. Try it as a marinade for pressed extra-firm tofu, or as a stir-fry sauce for noodles and vegetables.

Yield: 2 cups

Prep time: 10 minutes | Total time: 10 minutes

1¼ cups freshly squeezed orange juice
¼ cup rice vinegar
⅓ cup soy sauce
1 teaspoon toasted sesame oil
1 tablespoon minced fresh ginger
4 medium cloves garlic, minced
½ teaspoon onion powder
½ teaspoon agave

In a medium bowl, whisk together all the ingredients. Use the marinade immediately.

My Tips

Pico de Gallo

This simple salsa made with fresh ingredients is a true Mexican classic. It's the ideal accompaniment to tortilla chips, and it adds authentic flavor to nearly any Mexican dish. Use it to top our Beefy Tacos (page 84), to season our Breakfast Burrito (page 26), and to liven up our Nacho Cheese Sauce (page 137).

Yield: 1½ cups

Prep time: 10 minutes | Total time: 10 minutes

1 cup diced tomatoes
¼ cup diced red onion
1 medium jalapeño, seeded and diced
2 medium cloves garlic, minced
½ cup chopped fresh cilantro
Juice of ½ lime

In a small bowl, combine all the ingredients and mix well. Enjoy fresh or store in a sealed container in the refrigerator for up to 3 days.

My Tips

Caesar Dressing

Forget raw eggs and anchovies. This plant-based Caesar dressing brings all the flavor of the original, without making you feel like you're missing anything, which is what we're all about. This recipe comes from our insanely talented friend Allison Rivers Samson and was featured in *The Dairy-Freedom Cookbook* that we wrote together.

Like us, you might enjoy making batches of this dressing to keep on hand for salads throughout the week. It's a cinch to make and infinitely better than store-bought dressing.

Yield: 1 cup

Prep time: 10 minutes | Total time: 10 minutes

You'll need: a blender

½ cup olive oil
½ cup canola oil
4 large cloves garlic, peeled
¼ cup freshly squeezed lemon juice
1 sheet sushi nori (roasted seaweed), hand-crushed into tiny flakes (about 4 teaspoons)
4 teaspoons capers
1½ teaspoons salt
1 teaspoon ground black pepper
1 teaspoon Dijon mustard

In a blender, blend all the ingredients until a creamy dressing forms. Use the dressing immediately or store it in a glass jar in the fridge for up to 1 week.

Why It Works: The oils and lemon juice blend together to create an emulsion that makes this dressing creamy without eggs.

My Tips

Strawberry Preserves

This takes just a few minutes to make, requires only three ingredients, and features one of our favorite fruits: the strawberry. You don't have to wait for strawberry season to make this, though; we use frozen strawberries so we can enjoy it all year round. Try this simple recipe on Waffles (page 29) and Pancakes (page 33), and inside our delectable Toaster Pastries (page 30). We also like spooning these preserves over ice cream, stirring them into yogurt, and slathering them on toast.

Yield: 1½ cups

Prep time: 2 minutes | Cook time: 10 minutes | Total time: 12 minutes

1 (12-ounce) bag frozen strawberries
2 tablespoons granulated sugar
2 tablespoons chia seeds

1. In a small pot over medium heat, combine all the ingredients. Bring to a low boil and boil gently, uncovered, for 10 to 15 minutes, stirring frequently. As the strawberries soften, use a fork or potato masher to mash them to achieve your preferred amount of "chunkiness."

2. Remove the preserves from the heat. Serve immediately or store in an airtight glass container (such as a small mason jar) in the refrigerator for up to 5 days.

Friendly Suggestion: If you don't like strawberries, you can also use raspberries, blackberries, or blueberries.

My Tips

Basic Pizza Dough

Rejoice for the best pizza dough around, created by none other than the queen of vegan baking and our dear friend, Colleen Patrick-Goudreau. She is the author of the first vegan cookbook that either of us ever purchased, *The Joy of Vegan Baking*, and it's a real honor for us to include this recipe in our very own book more than a decade later. You can make any type of pizza with this basic dough, and the recipe can be doubled if you're feeding a crowd or want extra dough for freezing.

Colleen incorporates zero-waste practices into her home and has inspired us to do the same. Making your own staples (like pizza dough) is an effective way to cut down on plastic waste (especially if you buy your pantry items in bulk), while also saving money. So enjoy this dough that saves dough!

Yield: 2 pizza doughs

Prep time: 30 minutes + 2 hours for rising | Cook time: 20 minutes | Total time: 2 hours and 50 minutes

You'll need: an electric stand mixer with a dough hook (if using the mixer option)

1 cup warm water

1 envelope (2½ teaspoons) active dry yeast

1 tablespoon granulated sugar

3¼ cups all-purpose flour, divided

1 teaspoon salt

1 tablespoon olive oil, plus additional for greasing the bowl

1. Add 1 cup of warm water to a small bowl. The water should feel warm to your finger but not too hot—the temperature of a comfortable bath. Water that is too hot will kill the yeast; water that is too cold will not activate it.

2. Sprinkle the yeast into the water, add the sugar, and stir gently until they dissolve, about 1 minute. When the yeast is mixed with the water at the proper temperature, a smooth, beige mixture results.

3. Let the yeast mixture sit for 5 minutes; by this point, a thin layer of creamy foam should cover the surface, indicating that the yeast is effective. (Discard the mixture and start over with a fresh package of yeast if bubbles have not formed within 5 minutes.)

4. To prepare the dough, feel free to mix by hand or using a stand mixer. The directions for each are below.

Mixing your dough by hand:

1. In a large bowl, combine 3 cups of the flour with the salt. Make a well in the center of the flour and pour in the yeast mixture and the oil. Using a wooden spoon, vigorously stir the flour into the well, beginning in the center and working toward the sides of the bowl, until the flour is incorporated and the soft dough just begins to hold together.

2. Turn the dough out onto a lightly floured surface. Dust your hands with flour and knead the dough gently in the following manner: Press down on the dough with the heels of your hands and push it away from you, then partially fold it back over itself. Shift it a quarter turn and repeat the procedure. While kneading, very gradually add just enough of the remaining ¼ cup of flour until the dough is no longer sticky or tacky; this should take about 5 minutes. As you work, use a metal dough scraper to pry up any bits of dough that stick to the work surface. Continue kneading until the dough is smooth, elastic, and shiny, 10 to 15 minutes longer. Knead the dough only until it feels smooth and springy; too much kneading overdevelops the gluten in the flour and results in a tough crust.

Mixing your dough with a stand mixer:

1. In the bowl of a stand mixer, combine 3 cups of the flour and the salt, yeast mixture, and oil. Attach the dough hook and beat on low speed until well mixed, about 1 minute. Switch to medium speed and beat until the dough is smooth and elastic, about 5 minutes. If the dough is sticky, continue kneading while gradually adding just enough of the remaining ¼ cup of flour for the dough to lose its stickiness. If the dough is dry and crumbly, add warm water, 1 tablespoon at a time, until the dough is smooth and elastic.

---

5. After mixing and kneading the dough, shape it into a ball and place it in a well-oiled bowl, turning to coat completely on all sides with oil. (This oiling of the dough prevents a hard surface from forming that would inhibit rising.) Cover the bowl tightly with plastic wrap and drape a towel over the top of the covered bowl.

6. Set the dough aside to rise in a draft-free warm place until doubled in bulk, about 1½ to 2 hours.
7. As soon as the dough has doubled in bulk, use your fist to punch it down to prevent overrising. Squeeze the dough into a ball, pressing out all the air bubbles. If you cannot bake the pizza dough within 2 hours of its rising, punch down the dough, turn it in an oiled bowl to coat once more, cover the bowl tightly with plastic wrap, and refrigerate. (The dough can be kept refrigerated for up to 36 hours before the yeast is exhausted and the dough becomes unusable.) Let the chilled dough come to room temperature before proceeding.
8. To make one 15- to 16-inch pizza, keep the dough in a single ball. To make two 12-inch pizzas or two 9-inch deep-dish pizzas, divide the dough into 2 pieces. To make individual 9-inch pizzas, divide the dough into 4 to 6 equal portions. To make appetizer-sized pizzas, divide the dough into 12 to 18 equal portions. Once you prepare your pizza, bake for 18 to 20 minutes.
9. If you wish to freeze the dough for later use, wrap the pieces tightly in plastic wrap or seal in freezer bags or airtight plastic containers and freeze for up to 4 months. Before using, thaw in the refrigerator for 1 to 2 days or for a few hours at room temperature.

My Tips

_____

_____

_____

Overnight Sourdough Bread

Toni makes a sourdough loaf nearly every week using this recipe from our dear friend Kristie Middleton, who is the author of the book *Meatless*. It'll require a sourdough starter, which you can get from a friend, make using an online recipe, or even purchase online (for example, from Amazon). Here's what Kristie has to say about the recipe: "I took a sourdough class a couple of years ago and it's changed my life. I love baking and always have a fresh loaf on hand. It's much easier to make than you'd think. Here's how to make easy, delicious no-knead overnight sourdough bread."

Yield: 1 loaf

Prep time: 20 minutes + 12 hours for rising | Cook time: 40 minutes | Total time: 1 hour +

12 hours for rising

Advance prep required (feed sourdough starter 4 hours before making the dough)

3¾ cups all-purpose flour
1 teaspoon salt
½ cup sourdough starter
that has been fed at
least 4 hours prior to
making the dough
1½ cups water

1. In a large bowl, combine the flour and salt, then add the starter and water. Mix well. The dough should be sticky enough to form a ball. Add additional water if needed to form a ball, 1 tablespoon at a time.

2. Cover the bowl with a towel and allow the dough to rise for 8 to 18 hours; 12 hours is the sweet spot.

3. Preheat the oven to 500 degrees F and place a Dutch oven inside.

4. Meanwhile, on a floured surface, stretch the dough into a rectangle. Fold the corners into each other, roll over and tuck to form a ball. Using a knife, lightly slice an X into the top of the ball of dough (or get creative with your own designs). Allow to rest until the oven has reached 500 degrees F.

5. Carefully place the ball of dough in the hot Dutch oven and cover with the lid. Bake for 30 minutes.

6. Remove the lid, reduce the heat to 450 degrees F, and bake for an additional 5 to 10 minutes, depending on the desired darkness of the bread.

Friendly Suggestion: We recommend feeding your starter at least once a week. To feed, start with 1 tablespoon of starter and add ⅓ cup of flour and slightly less than ⅓ cup of water. Mix together. Allow the starter to rest for 4 to 6 hours prior to baking. Keep in the refrigerator if not baking.

My Tips

_____

_____

_____

Cornbread

If you're a fan of classic cornbread, you'll love this recipe. It's super easy to prepare (we're talkin' like fifteen minutes until it's in the oven), and guaranteed to bring nostalgic comfort to your kitchen. For a warming meal on a cold winter's night, serve this cornbread with Our Favorite Chili (page 115) and sliced avocado, and boom! You're in for a real treat.

Yield: 10 servings

Prep time: 15 minutes | Cook time: 20 minutes | Total time: 35 minutes

2 tablespoons ground flaxseed meal

¼ cup plus 1 tablespoon water

1 cup all-purpose flour

1 cup cornmeal

1 tablespoon plus 1 teaspoon baking powder

½ cup granulated sugar

1 teaspoon salt

¼ cup canola oil

1 cup unsweetened, plain soy milk

1. Preheat the oven to 425 degrees F. Lightly grease an 8-inch cast-iron skillet (or 8-inch round cake pan).

2. In a small bowl, whisk together the flaxseed meal and water. Set aside for 5 minutes.

3. In a large bowl, combine the flour, cornmeal, baking powder, sugar, and salt.

4. Pour the canola oil, soy milk, and flaxseed meal mixture into the large bowl, and mix by hand until combined.

5. Pour the batter into the prepared skillet (or pan) and bake for 20 minutes. Remove from the oven and use a toothpick to poke the middle of the cornbread. If it comes out smooth, allow to cool. If it comes out with batter, return the cornbread to the oven and bake for 5 more minutes.

6. Allow the cornbread to cool for 30 minutes before serving.

Friendly Suggestion: Level up your cornbread by adding ¼ cup of fresh, frozen, or canned corn kernels to your batter before baking.

My Tips

Dinner Rolls

Baking from scratch can be daunting for the uninitiated, but these biscuit-like dinner rolls are beginner-friendly. Plus, pulling apart warm homemade dinner rolls is totally worth it—we promise! Serve these with vegan butter, or for something extra decadent, with our savory Mushroom Gravy (page 231).

Yield: 15 rolls

Prep time: 30 minutes + 1 hour for rising | Cook time: 20 minutes | Total time: 1 hour and 50 minutes

You'll need: an electric stand mixer with a dough hook (if using the mixer option)

4½ cups all-purpose flour, divided
2 tablespoons active dry yeast
¼ cup granulated sugar
1 teaspoon salt
¼ cup plus 1 tablespoon vegan butter
1½ cups unsweetened, plain soy milk
1 tablespoon melted vegan butter

Directions if using a stand mixer:

1. In the bowl of a stand mixer with a dough hook, combine 3 cups of the flour and the yeast, sugar, and salt.

2. In a small microwave-safe bowl, microwave the vegan butter and soy milk for 1 minute. Stir until the butter is completely melted and the mixture is combined. The mixture should be lukewarm. If you have a food thermometer, it should register 105 to 110 degrees F. Pour the butter mixture into the stand mixer bowl.

3. Turn the mixer on the lowest speed and mix for 2 minutes. Scrape the sides of the bowl and add the remaining 1½ cups of flour. Continue mixing (kneading) on low for 2 more minutes. Increase to medium speed and mix for 1 more minute. If you notice that the bowl still has loose, dry ingredients, hand-knead them into the dough ball, then continue with the dough hook.

4. Lightly oil a large bowl. Place the ball of dough in the bowl, cover with a damp towel, and allow to rise for 30 minutes at room temperature.

5. Lightly oil a 9 × 13-inch baking pan. Pinch off 15 equal-sized balls of dough and place them on the

pan. Cover the dough balls with a damp towel and allow them to rise for 30 minutes.

6. Preheat the oven to 375 degrees F. Bake the rolls for 18 to 20 minutes, until they turn light brown.

7. Brush the melted vegan butter over the tops of the dinner rolls.

Directions if mixing by hand:

1. In a large bowl, mix together 3 cups of the flour and the yeast, sugar, and salt until combined.

2. In a small microwave-safe bowl, microwave the vegan butter and soy milk for 1 minute. Stir until the butter is completely melted and the mixture is combined. The mixture should be lukewarm. If you have a food thermometer, it should register 105 to 110 degrees F. Pour the butter mixture into the large bowl of dry ingredients and mix with a fork until combined.

3. Slowly add the remaining 1½ cups of flour while kneading with your hands for 5 minutes or until all the flour is incorporated and the dough is smooth.

4. Lightly oil a large bowl. Place the ball of dough in the bowl, cover with a damp towel, and allow to rise for 30 minutes at room temperature.

5. Lightly oil a 9 × 13-inch baking pan. Pinch off 15 equal-sized balls of dough and place them on the pan. Cover the dough balls with a damp towel and allow them to rise for 30 minutes.

6. Preheat the oven to 375 degrees F. Bake the rolls for 18 to 20 minutes, until they turn light brown.

7. Brush the melted vegan butter over the dinner rolls.

My Tips

Challah

We love making homemade challah to enjoy for our Shabbat dinners, especially when we have family or friends over. There is something about the communal tearing of bread (which is the traditional way Jewish people enjoy challah—passing it around the table and tearing off pieces) that brings a connectedness to any gathering. Try toasting it the next morning and topping with some vegan butter or jelly. So good! And when the challah begins to harden after a couple of days (if it lasts that long), we love making it into Challah French Toast (page 39).

This recipe—with a few adaptations of our own—comes from the kitchen of Rebecca Moreno, who used to run the all-vegan Harm Less Bakery in Oakland, California. Shabbat shalom!

Yield: 1 loaf

Prep time: 40 minutes + 2 hours and 20 minutes for rising | Cook time: 40 minutes | Total time: 3 hours

1 cup + 3 tablespoons water

1 teaspoon plus ½ cup granulated sugar, divided

2½ teaspoons active dry yeast

¼ cup plus 2 tablespoons refined coconut oil

4 cups all-purpose flour, divided

2 teaspoons baking powder

2 teaspoons salt

¼ teaspoon ground turmeric

2 tablespoons agave

1 tablespoon sesame seeds or poppy seeds

1. In a small microwave-safe bowl, warm the water in the microwave for about 1 minute. (It should be warm but not hot to the touch; if you have a food thermometer, it should register 105 to 110 degrees F.) Sprinkle in 1 teaspoon of the sugar and swirl it around so it dissolves. Lightly sprinkle the yeast into the sugar water and allow the yeast to awaken for 7 minutes.

2. In another small microwave-safe bowl, heat the coconut oil in the microwave for 30 seconds or just long enough to bring it to a liquid state. Set aside.

3. In a large bowl, combine 2 cups of the flour with the remaining ½ cup of sugar, baking powder, salt, and turmeric and mix with a fork.

4. Add the yeast mixture and melted coconut oil to the dry ingredient mixture and stir until combined. Slowly add the remaining 2 cups of flour and, using your hands, knead the dough

for a full 10 minutes, until all the flour is incorporated and you have a smooth dough.

5. Grease a large bowl. Place the dough ball in the bowl, cover loosely with a damp towel, place in a warm area (such as near the oven or in the sun), and allow to rise for about 1½ hours.

6. After the time has passed, very lightly flour a flat surface and roll your risen dough into a long, thick snake 14 to 16 inches long. To make a classic three-strand braid, cut the dough into equal thirds. Starting in the center of the dough piece and using your hands to gently roll outward, roll each piece into a strand that is 12 to 14 inches long with the ends slightly tapered. Once all three dough pieces are rolled out, bring one end of each strand together and massage them firmly together to stick. Just as in a traditional braid, bring the left strand over the center one, making the left strand the new center strand. Then bring the right strand over the center strand, making that the new center strand. Repeat this pattern (left to center, right to center, and so on) until you reach the end of your strands. Press the ends together and tuck them under the end of your loaf. Go back and tuck the top of the loaf as well to produce rounded ends.

7. Line a baking sheet with parchment paper or a silicone mat. Place your loaf on the baking sheet, cover with a damp towel, and allow to rise for another 50 minutes.

8. Preheat the oven to 350 degrees F.

9. Once your loaf is looking nice and puffy, remove the cloth. Using a basting brush, lightly spread the agave evenly across the entire loaf, including the sides. Sprinkle the loaf with the sesame or poppy seeds. Bake for 35 to 40 minutes, until the top is hardened and a rich golden brown.

10. Allow to fully cool before wrapping with a challah cover or towel. Tear (or slice) and enjoy!

Friendly Suggestion: Challah freezes beautifully. Slice the loaf before popping it into the freezer so you can pull out a slice to toast whenever the fancy strikes.

My Tips

_____

_____

Friendly Vegan
Menus

We love hosting gatherings for our family and friends, and we've gotten a lot of experience with it lately while planning house-warmings, baby showers, and wedding rehearsal dinners (life has been busy for us lately!). We've compiled the top recipes that our guests always rave about and included them in three menus for special occasions.

Planning a party is tough work, so let us lighten your load with party favorites that everyone is guaranteed to love.

Dinner Party

We love a good dinner party! The intimacy of gathering with friends over a home-cooked meal is central to many of our best memories. When we became vegan in college, we prepared meals for our loved ones in our dorms and tiny apartments, with our guests sitting on the floor to eat. It helped us understand that regardless of the setting, good food and conversation is the foundation of a really fantastic experience. Whether you're dining on the floor or at an elegantly decorated dinner table, this menu sets the stage for an especially memorable dinner party, we promise.

Our dream dinner party kicks off with an appetizer of flavorful pesto crostini topped with colorful cherry tomatoes. For the entrée, we bring out our favorite recipe in the book—fettuccine Alfredo garnished with fresh parsley. On the side, we love serving up southern collard greens, Caesar salad, and a basket of sliced sourdough bread. Although your guests will surely be full, one can always make room for little ramekins of our delicate chocolate mousse decorated with a dollop of vegan whipped cream (or our Strawberry Preserves, page 245) and a sprig of mint. Invite us, please!

On the menu:

Pesto Crostini (page 147)

Classic Caesar Salad (page 157)

Fettuccine Alfredo (page 75)

Michael's Southern Collard
Greens (page 154)

Overnight Sourdough Bread
(page 249)

Chocolate Mousse (page 199)

Friendly Vegan Barbecue

We're very laid-back gals, so we often turn to the backyard barbecue to celebrate special occasions. We appreciate the ease and the casual atmosphere for our guests, and it's an awesome way to make the most of summer while appreciating time outdoors.

We are both big fans of the latest and greatest vegan burgers and hot dogs on the market, so we usually buy those and then make a bunch of side dishes. But we're also including our black bean burger recipe on this menu in case you want to go the fully homemade route.

Friendly Vegan Holiday Feast

The holidays provide a wonderful opportunity to share vegan comfort food with your friends and loved ones. We've both hosted Thanksgiving dinners on countless occasions (last year we hosted three!), and we've discovered which dishes our guests love most.

We designed this menu to include a filling array of dishes that are rich, creamy, savory, and sweet, to complement your centerpiece (we love serving store-bought vegan roasts). If you don't tell anyone, your guests probably won't even notice that these dishes are vegan!

Our Tips for Dining as a Friendly Vegan Guest

Hosting a meal is a special experience because you're able to control the entire menu and showcase some of the best plant-based foods. But when you're a *guest* at dinner parties, potlucks, and gatherings, you can still make sure you always have something to eat (and spread some plant-based love around) by bringing a dish to share. Here are five of our favorite dishes to bring to gatherings:

Lasagna (page 60)

Pesto Pasta (page 81)

Cornbread Chili Casserole
  (page 82)

Stephanie's Deviled Potatoes
  (page 141)

Fudgy Brownies (page 186)

Acknowledgments

This cookbook wouldn't exist without the following people. We are extremely grateful to all of you!

Michelle's Acknowledgments

To my little bear, Graham, who was growing in my belly throughout the writing of this book, giving little kicks that brought me the biggest smiles— even when I was on version five of a recipe that still wasn't perfect. I love you.

To my hubby, Dan, who patiently endured many late nights, taste tested almost all of the recipes in this book, cleaned more dishes than I can count, and even made some of the recipes when I had such bad morning sickness I could barely bring myself to open the fridge.

To my mom and dad, who supported me when I decided to go vegetarian when I was just eight years old, again when I became vegan in college, and again when I decided to write this book.

To the Millers, and Heather and Holly, who so warmly welcomed me into the family without ever making me feel alienated for being an herbivore, and quickly got to work veganizing family favorites.

To my birth father, Greg Hicks, for tirelessly recipe testing with me and being the first to volunteer every time I needed help. It breaks my heart that you won't get to see this book come to life, but your passion for epic vegan food will be eternally remembered in the pages within.

To my Hicks family for sharing your love of cooking, and to Grandma, Barbara Hicks, for sharing your beloved cookie recipe (page 179).

To my birth mother for passing on the compassion gene and the love for animals that is so core to who I am today. And to my vegetable-hating brother, for reminding me how much work there is still to be done in the world (wink wink).

To Toni, who is so much more than a coauthor, for being the highest-caliber friend, for always keeping it real, and for making us the best soups on planet Earth when life gets hard.

To Beatriz, who not only was instrumental in the making of this cook-book but also has become a truly lifesaving work partner and an essential part of World of Vegan.

Finally, I want to share a special note of gratitude with my readers at World of Vegan, my @Vegan Instagram family, my YouTube community, my podcast listeners, and anyone else I've had the privilege of connecting with through the power of the internet. Thank you for inviting me into your world. You give me purpose, and it's my greatest joy to be a friendly vegan by your side as you venture along an increasingly kind and con-scious path.

Toni's Acknowledgments

I am grateful to my husband, Paul Shapiro, who is the most generous and supportive partner I could be blessed to have in my life. At this point, we've shared six months of marriage, and in that time you've supported me as I've traveled weekly to promote my book *Plant-Based on a Budget* and spent any other spare moments writing and recipe testing for this book. I recognize and appreciate how you accommodate me, and I love that you encourage me to live my passion for helping people and animals, and even more, I'm glad that you live it, too.

Thank you to my family, George and Lisa Okamoto, Gabriel Okamoto, Elena Deras, and Larry and Jolene Shapiro, for all the love you constantly send my way. I feel it strongly and it drives me every day.

To Michelle, thank you for accommodating my inability to work before noon and for realizing that when I'm getting cranky it's probably because I'm hungry or sleepy. I appreciate you and our friendship more than I can ever express, and I'm glad we're on this path together.

To my Plant-Based on a Budget team, Bea Buono-Core, Deanne Thomsen, and Alfonso Revilla: I'm so grateful for all the care and attention to detail that you put into Plant-Based on a Budget. Your help is so immensely appreciated, and I'll always be grateful to you guys for holding down the fort while I took time off to write this book. You're more than colleagues to me, and I'm honored to know each of you on a personal level and to be inspired by your dedication and compassion.

Lastly, dear Plant-Based on a Budget audience, supporting you is how I want to spend the rest of my life. Thank you for virtually sharing your stories with me and allowing me to be part of your journey. I read every comment, message, email, book review, and so on that you send my way. I see you and you matter to me.

I'm so privileged to have a community and support system that props me up and gives me so much love and encouragement—the depth of my gratitude reaches down to my core. Thank you, thank you, thank you!

Combined Acknowledgments

Thank you to all of the friends and family over the years who have inspired us in our own cooking, several of whom we've included recipes from in this book: Zhoro Apostolov, Grandma Florence Cehn, Kathy Chrzaszcz,

Stephanie Dreyer, Grandma Barbara Hicks, Greg Hicks, Kristie Middleton, Rebecca Moreno (Harm Less Bakery), Colleen Patrick-Goudreau, Jen Regan, Allison Rivers Samson, Jolene Shapiro, Michael Wallace, and Jennifer Wong. We learned to cook by cooking with friends and for friends, and each of those gatherings and experiences played a little part in what this book became today.

To our agents, Anna Petkovich and Celeste Fine, thank you for taking us under your wings and making us feel supported throughout this cookbook journey. To our publisher, Glenn Yeffeth, thank you for investing in us and making us feel valued as authors. At BenBella you've created a powerhouse team who have made us feel like we are all equally on this journey together. To our editor, Claire Schulz, thank you for bringing to life our ideas, for the many Skype brainstorming calls, and for truly collaborating with us on this project. To Aurelia for enhancing our writing and bringing even more personality to our book. To our marketing manager, Heather Butterfield, we can't thank you enough for the amount of care and thought you bring to sharing our book with the world. We value you professionally, but we're also grateful you've become our friend. To Sarah Avinger and the design team, to Monica Lowry in production, and to everyone else at BenBella who has been on this journey with us. Thank you for providing us with such great guidance, advice, and support so that our cookbook became as beautiful and helpful to people as the recipes are delicious.

To our recipe photographer, Zhoro Apostolov, who has been working with both of us since long before this book project to make vegan food look delicious on both Plant-Based on a Budget and World of Vegan: we're so grateful to you for capturing each and every one of our recipes in this book so beautifully through your lens. And to our lifestyle photographer, Lauren Alisse White, thank you for bringing life, energy, and warmth to this cookbook and making us feel so comfortable in front of the camera.

Thank you to Beatriz Buono-Core for . . .where do we begin? For everything. Without you, this book would not be the book it is today. Thank you for helping with our recipe testers, for cooking up many of the meals in this book yourself, and for helping with keeping World of Vegan and Plant-Based on a Budget running while we were focused on writing this book. We feel so supported by you and grateful to have you by our side throughout this project.

Thank you to our incredible team of nearly seventy-five recipe testers, who helped us make sure every single recipe is delicious, foolproof, and the very best it can be: Grace Amico, Beth Arnold, Justin Au, Linda Babin, Melissa Balick, Toube Benedetto, Nicole Benson, Max Broad, Karen Brockway, Anita Bröllochs, Beatriz Buono-Core, Heather Butterfield, Jenna Cameron, Yolanda Calderón, Gianna Cannataro, Brian Cassidy, Sharlene Cassidy, Joan Cehn, Laura Cheneliam, Diane Cheng, Isabelle Cnudde, Lisa Colvin, Janet Cooper, Margaret Curtis, Bill Dendle, Steve Erlsten, Annemieke Farrow, Mary K Ferreter, Jodie Foreman, Shana Franklin, Caryn Ginsberg, Ruth Havertz, Tony Held, Patty Henrichsen, Greg Hicks, Logan Jeffrey, Jenny B. Jones, Lain Kahlstrom, Carrie Lande, Megan Lindeman, Virginia Loenberg, Susan Malphurs, Amanda Mann, Roxane Masson, Wendy McMillan, Carol Messina, Lisa Okamoto, Jenny Ortega, Jennifer Piccolo, Kim Ponce, Jackie Poles Ran, Emily Clark Rogers, Michelle Rosier, Darren Roth, Michelle Salemi, Nate Salpeter, Taylor Schoendorf, Jolene Shapiro, Paul Shapiro, Kristen Sinch, Sarah Smith, Melanie Swanson, Breege Tomkinson, Lisa Towell, Elisabeth Trotter, Debbie Tsujimoto, Rebecca Tuohino, Cheri Turner, Sandra Vu, Michael Wallace, Andrea Waybright, Taylor Wolfram, Heather Zehel, and Brian Zimmer.

And finally, to all of you reading this now, thank you for giving this book a chance.

Friendly Vegan
Resources

The Plant-Powered People Podcast | PlantPoweredPodcast.com
Life is always easier and more exciting when you have friends to share your journey. On our podcast, *The Plant-Powered People Podcast*, we chat with folks who've embraced plant-based living while they share their experiences overcoming obstacles in the most graceful (and sometimes not-so-graceful) ways. Tune in on iTunes, Spotify, or wherever you listen to podcasts.

Plant-Based on a Budget Meal Plans | PlantBasedMealPlan.com

Eating healthfully doesn't need to be expensive. In fact, delicious plant-based meals that are packed with protein, fiber, disease-fighting nutrients, and lots of flavor can be super-affordable and easy to make. Our meticulously crafted and beautifully designed meal plans show you how to hack the supermarket so that you can get all the food you'll want for an entire week for a grocery bill of only $25 (that's just $1.20 per meal).

7 Days Documentary | 7DaysDoc.com

In our very first mini-documentary, we follow twenty-three-year-old Raul Medina as he swaps his fast-food diet for whole foods for one week. You won't believe how just seven days of plant-based eating transformed his life.

Vegan YouTube Videos | YouTube.com/WorldofVegan

Subscribe to watch weekly vegan food and lifestyle videos covering every topic you can imagine in an upbeat and friendly way. You'll find recipe videos, food hauls, "What I Eat in a Day" videos, and beyond.

Budget Vegan Recipes | PlantBasedonaBudget.com

There are a lot of reasons to eat more plants, and a lot of misconceptions about what that means. The goal behind the Plant-Based on a Budget website is to offer recipes and meal plans that show how affordable, easy, and delicious eating a plant-based diet can be; how you don't have to shop at specialty grocery stores or restock your pantry with all kinds of unfamiliar products and substitutes; and, most of all, how you don't have to sacrifice time, taste, or money in the pursuit of healthier, tastier eating.

Vegan Food & Lifestyle Website | WorldofVegan.com

Michelle's website, World of Vegan, is a one-stop spot to find delicious vegan recipes, helpful vegan guides, informative articles, and fun videos. You'll also get a weekly dose of inspiration in your email inbox if you sign up for the World of Vegan newsletter.

Plant-Based on a Budget cookbook

Toni's book *Plant-Based on a Budget* gives you one hundred inexpensive recipes and a detailed meal plan to make plant-based eating easy, accessible, and, most of all, affordable. Like *The Friendly Vegan Cookbook*, each recipe includes beautiful photos and plenty of helpful lifestyle tips.

The 12-Day Dairy Detox | TheDairyDetox.com

The 12-Day Dairy Detox course is designed to get you started with vegan living. You can look forward to delicious plant-based recipes, two weeks of daily videos, a sample meal plan, time-saving tips, and more that will help you on your path to dairy freedom and feeling your best.

Connect With Toni:

- @plantbasedonabudget
- @plantbasedblog
- Pinterest.com/toniokamoto
- Facebook.com/ PlantBasedonaBudget

Connect With Michelle:

- @vegan / @michellecehn
- @worldofvegan / @michellecehn
- Pinterest.com/worldofvegan
- Facebook.com/worldofvegan

Metric Conversions

Volume Equivalents (Liquid)

Standard	US Standard (Ounces)	Metric (Approximate)
2 tablespoons	1 fl. oz.	30 mL
¼ cup	2 fl. oz.	60 mL
½ cup	4 fl. oz.	120 mL
1 cup	8 fl. oz.	240 mL
1½ cups	12 fl. oz.	355 mL
2 cups or 1 pint	16 fl. oz.	475 mL
4 cups or 1 quart	32 fl. oz.	1 L
1 gallon	128 fl. oz.	4 L

Volume Equivalents (Dry)

Standard	Metric (Approximate)
⅛ teaspoon	0.5 mL
¼ teaspoon	1 mL
½ teaspoon	2 mL
¾ teaspoon	4 mL
1 teaspoon	5 mL
1 tablespoon	15 mL
¼ cup	59 mL
⅓ cup	79 mL
½ cup	118 mL
⅔ cups	158 mL
¾ cup	177 mL
1 cup	237 mL
2 cups or 1 pint	475 mL
3 cups	700 mL
4 cups or 1 quart	1 L

Weight Equivalents

Standard	Metric (Approximate)
½ ounce	15 g
1 ounce	30 g
2 ounces	60 g
4 ounces	115 g
8 ounces	225 g
12 ounces	340 g
16 ounces or 1 pound	455 g

Oven Temperatures

Fahrenheit (F)	Celsius (C) (Approximate)
250°	120°
300°	150°
325°	165°
350°	180°
375°	190°
400°	205°
425°	220°
450°	230°

Subject Index

Recipe and Ingredient Index

About the Authors

Toni Okamoto is the founder of Plant-Based on a Budget, the popular website and meal plan that shows you how to save dough by eating veggies. She's also the author of the *Plant-Based on a Budget* cookbook and *The Super Easy Vegan Slow Cooker Cookbook* and the cohost of *The Plant-Powered People Podcast*. Toni's work has been profiled by NBC News and *Parade* magazine, and she's a regular presence on local and national morning shows across the country, where she teaches viewers how to break their meat habit without breaking their budget. She was also featured in the popular documentary *What the Health*. When she's not cooking up a plant-based storm, she's spending time with her husband and their newly rescued dog in Sacramento, California.

Michelle Cehn is the founder of the internationally acclaimed food and lifestyle website World of Vegan, runs the popular Instagram channel @Vegan, and is a YouTube personality who has reached millions through her creative and relatable vegan videos. Michelle is an avid food photographer and filmmaker, and, along with Toni, she cohosts *The Plant-Powered People Podcast*, creates celebrated plant-based meal plans, and produced the mini-documentary *7 Days*. When she's not creating plant-based resources and celebrating vegan food, you'll find her floating down the river, running, cooking, and stepping into mom life with her husband, plant-powered dog, and little newborn son in sunny California.

Download a **FREE** digital copy of
BenBella's Best of Plant-Based Eating
and sign up for more
exclusive offers and info at
BENBELLAVEGAN.COM

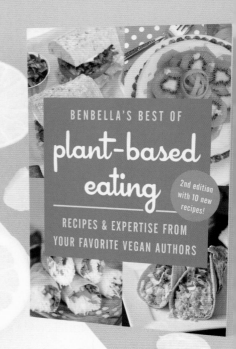

WITH NEARLY 50 RECIPES FROM

The China Study cookbook series | Lindsay S. Nixon's The Happy Herbivore series
Chef Del Sroufe's *Better Than Vegan* | Christy Morgan's *Blissful Bites*
Heather Crosby's *YumUniverse* | Tracy Russell's *The Best Green Smoothies on the Planet*
Dreen Burton's *Plant-Powered Families* | Jeff and Joan Stanford's *Dining at The Ravens*
Eric Brent and Glen Merzer's *The HappyCow Cookbook*
Laura Theodore's *Jazzy Vegetarian Classics* | Christina Ross' *Love Fed*
Kim Campbell's *The PlantPure Nation Cookbook*

AND SELECTIONS FROM

T. Colin Campbell and Howard Jacobsons' *Whole* and *The Low-Carb Fraud*
Dr. Pam Popper and Glen Merzer's *Food Over Medicine*
J. Morris Hicks' *Healthy Eating, Healthy World* | Lani Muelrath's *The Plant-Based Journey*

BENBELLA
vegan

My Notes

My Notes

My Notes

My Notes